Praise for

AN AUTHENTIC SUCCESS

"I related to Authentic Success in many ways. Like most people, I spent much of my career being "reasonable" and "responsible"—making choices that delivered stability and the outward signs of success, often at the cost of personal fulfillment. By conventional standards, I had succeeded. Internally, something was missing.

What I learned is that fulfillment and financial success are not mutually exclusive. Achieving both is difficult, but possible. As Chad explains so clearly, real success comes from aligning your work with your values and purpose. Sometimes that alignment requires stepping down before moving forward—creating space for new paths and possibilities that weren't visible before.

I believe in doing hard things, because difficulty builds resilience and clarity. In my mid-fifties, I chose to leave a senior career to pursue a new entrepreneurial chapter. I did it to prove—to myself and to my children—that it's sometimes okay to be seen as "irresponsible" in order to live in alignment with what matters most.

There is never a convenient time to bet on yourself. Personal agency is real, and fear is not a reason to settle. The dreams worth pursuing are still out there—waiting for you to choose them."

Tim Rood. Founder / CEO Impact Capitol, National Speaker, Long time guest on CNBC, FOX Business News, Bloomberg TV

"An Authentic Success cuts through the noise of motivational hype and delivers something far more valuable: clarity. Chad Betz provides a grounded, experience-driven roadmap for professionals who have done 'everything right' yet still feel unfulfilled. This book challenges conventional definitions of success and replaces them with a practical framework for renewed purpose, momentum, and results."

Ford Saeks, CEO Prime Concepts Group, Inc.

"Chad Betz dismantles the most destructive myth plaguing high-achievers: that success has an expiration date. As a executive coach, Chad understands what I've seen in 30+ years of practice - limiting beliefs are the real barrier to success. This book provides the roadmap and tools professionals need to escape the 'Frustration Energy Cycle' and reclaim their authentic path to success—at any age."

Dr. Pat Boulogne, DC, CCSP, AP, CFMP, CEO, Elevare Advisory Group LLC, Performance Optimization Strategist

"Chad's book is a real life experience of how to recreate yourself and strive for success after 40. The book hits home for me as I too started a new company at 49 years old building it from 6 employees to 1400 and selling it to private equity. Chad describes the high's and low's of recreating yourself, and it's straight to the heart incorporating many lessons learned along the way."

Larry Chiavaro, LC Advisors Group LLC

Chad Reminds Us of What's Really Important
"This is the book I wish more mid-career professionals or better yet, seniors executives would read before they decide they're 'too late. There are countless stories of people who found a new mission or passion late in life. Stop wondering and take a step. Get this book!"

Darren LaCroix, CSP, AS, World Champion Speaker

"Chad Betz lays out a simple, actionable roadmap for getting unstuck, overcoming overwhelm, and rebuilding momentum! For example, I love his counterintuitive idea for getting inertia to work for you rather than against you. This is the no-excuses, no-fluff guide I wish I had years ago!"

Ed Tate, CSP—Certified Speaking ProfessionalWorld Champion of Public Speaking, Ed Tate & Associates

"Chad Betz writes with rare clarity, courage, and grounded wisdom. This book is not about quick wins or surface-level success — it's about alignment, responsibility, and choosing the kind of leadership that begins from the inside out. Chad challenges readers to tell themselves the truth, step into their vision, and lead with integrity in both business and life. This is a meaningful, practical read for anyone ready to move beyond potential and into purpose."

Joanne Victoria, Author & Speaker Truth Interrupted, ™
Author of *Vision With a Capital V: Create the Business of Your Dreams*

"An Authentic Success" delivers a refreshingly honest roadmap for professionals who feel they've missed their window for achievement. Chad Betz dismantles the myth that success has an expiration date while providing concrete tools for mindset shifts, habit formation, and strategic action. Drawing from his own crisis and transformation, Betz offers practical strategies rather than empty platitudes - from redefining success on your own terms to building genuine support systems and breaking the "Frustration Energy Cycle." This is more than motivation, it's a practical manual for anyone ready to stop second-guessing and start building the life they deserve.

Michael Davis, Author, *THE Book on Storytelling*
and *The Storytelling Power Trio*

"An Authentic Success punches a hole in the 'success-by-a-certain-age' illusion. Chad C. Betz reframes 'late' from a quiet fear into a real advantage—and gives you the push to build your next chapter on purpose. If you've been telling yourself the window closed, this book reopens it."

Ray Engan, Chief Charisma Creator, Leadership Through Laughter
Inventor of The Lean In Factor, The Humor Algorithm

"The definition of 'middle-aged' has changed, extending the old sell-by date for millions of professionals. Yet many outdated expectations still remain, creating friction in the workplace. Chad Betz offers a clear, practical roadmap for what comes next. An Authentic Success speaks directly to those who are still at the top of their game later in life."

Blaine Little, Author of The Communication Key & Corporate Trainer

"Chad Betz gets it: success doesn't expire just because you've hit a certain age. I built my consulting practice, then reinvented myself as a professional speaker because that was my dream, and I refused to let naysayers or self-doubt win.

Your best work isn't behind you; it's ahead, waiting for you to chase it. This book delivers practical strategies for your success, not empty motivation."
Gary McKinsey, Professional Speaker and Profit Strategist Leverage Your Competitive Advantage to Maintain Profitable Growth

"Chad Betz is in my Hall Of Fame as an individual who has demonstrated to me with commitment, hard work and a remarkable sensitivity to people you can take a God gifted skill of writing and make a significant difference in the life journey of people."
Fred Afragola, Founder, Frame Advisors, LLC

"If you're looking for a book to blow smoke up your ass, this isn't it. Chad presents the challenges in life from the perspective of a man who's been there, and is occasionally STILL there, while still working to be who he knows he can become. He offers practical exercises that are meant to keep you moving forward, if you're willing to let them."
Rich Hopkins, The WinAnyway Guy

"I love where he advises readers that a positive attitude is easy to have when everything's going your way; however, what happens when life gets in your way, or trips you up? I'm confident this book will help you!"
Tom Hill III, CCIM/SIOR, Tom Hill Realty & Investment

"Chad Betz delivers a thoughtful and encouraging message in An Authentic Success. The book is easy to read, relatable, and filled with practical insights for anyone who feels they may be behind in life or career. That, quite frankly, is a lot of people. This distraction culture, where people are always too busy to reflect and too busy fighting the fires of life and career, often sends us through time at warp speed. Chad Betz urges us to slow down so we can reflect, reinvent, and remove barriers at any age. A valuable reminder that progress is always possible for any of us if we start right now."
John M. O'Connor, President, Career Pro

AN AUTHENTIC SUCCESS

AN AUTHENTIC SUCCESS

YOU'RE NOT TOO OLD
AND IT'S NOT TOO LATE

CHAD BETZ

Published by HOBO Publishing

ISBN (paperback): 979-8-9851438-4-3
ISBN (ebook): 979-8-9851438-5-0

Book design and production by www.AuthorSuccess.com

Printed in the United States of America

Contents

Introduction

FAILURE! I was in my car, sitting in a parking garage under my office, staring blankly out the windshield at the wall. With the sounds of cars and the smell of exhaust in the background as people were leaving the office for the day, I was frozen, stuck in my head, wondering why, after all the work I had done in my life, I didn't feel like I had achieved anything. I felt tired, frustrated, and disheartened. I heard one word repeatedly screamed in my head: *FAILURE!*

At that point, I realized I had a decision to make. I needed to determine whether I was at my peak and ready to coast to the finish line, or whether I had more to give and was willing to put in extra work to achieve the success I always hoped for. I decided to push forward, to go out and work toward my goals. Although I didn't know it at the time, the incident in my car that day, fifteen years ago, was the beginning of the journey that led to this book.

Few things are as frustrating as being stuck in a rut, especially when your peers seem to be gaining the success you believe you should be achieving. Still, that frustration is not necessarily enough to motivate you to act. You may be hindered by the questions and self-doubt statements that can pop into your head.

Am I too old? I have a good job—What if I fail? My friends say I shouldn't rock the boat.

Am I too out of shape? Do I have the skills/ knowledge/technology prowess?

People can build inertia when they continue on a familiar path, even if it is not producing results. They keep going even if it is heading away from their goals. Even though it feels like you are making progress, it is like being on the wrong train. Each stop you pass brings you farther and farther from your goals. Luckily, with the tools in this book, you won't need to backtrack through each stop like the train. This book will help you renew your motivation and give you the tools to achieve the goals you may have given up on. You will get ideas and learn strategies to reset your thinking into a success mindset. Your time is ahead of you, not behind you.

You may compare yourself to your peers when you are gauging your success. The flaw in that comparison is the lack of complete information. You only see a part of their lives. You may see the vacation, but not the credit card bills and arguments over finances. When you look at people on social media, you never know whether things are exaggerated or even a lie. (Yes, people lie on social media about how great their life is.) By focusing on a skewed version of other people's success, you can lose focus on all of the things that you have accomplished and the assets you have right now to help you succeed. By taking an objective look at where you are now in terms of your definition of success, you can get to the starting line for your greatest level of success.

That objective look will probably show that you are not as far behind as you think. You have the skills you have learned and the experience you have gained. Your refocus on success does not make those assets go away.

The good news is that you have all the tools you need to succeed right now. Your tools may be a little out of use and rusty, but they're available to you. By reading this book, you will get the strategies you need to dust off those tools and put them to work for you. Once you have your toolbox working for you, you will learn the techniques for putting your tools into action so that you can reach a level of success you never imagined.

By reading this book, you will get:

§　**A Personal Framework for Success:** Techniques to redefine success on your own terms, not society's expectations.

§　**Tools to Escape Mediocrity:** Strategies to break out of stagnation and start living with purpose.

§　**A Roadmap to Overcome Real Obstacles:** Realistic responses to ageism, burnout, and lack of support.

§　**Support System Blueprint:** Ideas on cultivating a circle of people who support, not sabotage, your success.

§　**Action-Oriented Mindset:** This is not just a feel-good book. It is a call to action to adapt and move forward with the guidance you need to succeed!

I developed these strategies as I went through my own crisis. Through trial and error, then working with mentors and coaches, I was able to break free from self-doubt and self-imposed obstacles. The ideas were proven as I shared them with clients as a mentor and certified executive coach.

I went through what you are going through. I felt the frustration, embarrassment, anxiety, and despair. That experience, combined with the research and guidance I received, enabled me to develop these strategies, frameworks, and roadmaps. These tools help you bypass the discovery process I went through, allowing you to reach your goals more quickly.

Now that you've decided to succeed, let's look at the journey this book facilitates. The book is divided into four parts to guide you through the process of recognizing your ability to succeed and putting it into action.

§   **Section One: Late Doesn't Mean Too Late** helps you reflect on what success means to you and where you are in your success journey.

§   **Section Two: Develop Your Success Toolbox** introduces you to the tools in your toolbox and gives you techniques to improve them.

§   **Section Three: Using Your Success Toolbox** shows you how action is the key to success. Once you understand and improve your tools, this section gives you strategies for using these tools to LIVE THE LIFE YOU DESERVE!

You can feel isolated and overwhelmed when you try to succeed without guidance. It can feel like you have an impossible task in front of you. If you have ever walked through deep snow, you know it can be difficult. You need to lift your foot out of the snow and step, only for it to sink back to the bottom. When you have miles to walk, this can seem impossible. If someone else has done it before you, you get two benefits. One, you see that it is possible to succeed because someone else has done it. Two, your journey is easier because you can use that person's footsteps as a roadmap. You don't need to put in so much effort—you have a guide. This book offers those footsteps.

Now that you are about to begin your success journey, reflect on your professional and personal career. You probably see that you have accomplished things, but you may not be where you want to be at this point in your life. As you look back on your life, even if you feel it's too late to achieve your goals, this book is designed to help you reinvigorate your success journey so you can overcome your obstacles and celebrate your successes.

I hope you join me on this success journey. Success does not have an expiration date, and you are poised to be the success you've always dreamed of.

If you would like worksheets to help you document your plans, goals, and successes, go to:

www.AnAuthenticSuccess.com/tools
You're not too old, and it's not too late!

Late Doesn't Mean
Too Late

CHAPTER 1

Success Doesn't Have an Expiration Date!

*"You are never too old to set another goal
or to dream a new dream."*
–C.S. LEWIS

*"People are capable, at any time in their lives,
of doing what they dream of."*
–PAULO COELHO

An Authentic Success is a very personal journey, unique to you. There is a good chance that you put your Authentic Success aside to pursue society's version of success. When you are working toward society's success, you may find yourself burned out and unsatisfied. You may even reach a point where you believe you will never achieve your Authentic Success.

I found myself in this position. I had my idea of success influenced by '80s and '90s pop culture and movies. Striving for money and prestige while partying hard after hours. The company I worked for had a bar in the office. I worked hard, thinking I was succeeding, when in reality I was helping others achieve their goals at the expense of my own. This led to confusion and anxiety. I questioned why I was working so hard and not getting the rewards I had expected.

When you pursue other people's goals at the expense of your own, you can feel discouraged, anxious, and dissatisfied. You can end up looking back at decades of work that have only given you frustration. When that frustration shows, you may find yourself let go from your job, feeling discarded, and wondering if you have wasted your life.

Setbacks like a job loss can lead you to believe that your best years are behind you. Self-doubt and fears of failure can prevent you from taking the risks necessary to achieve success. This doubt and anxiety can be magnified through negative self-talk. The self-doubt that is generated by the negative self-talk can lead you to double down on society's version of success rather than trusting your ideas of success. The pressure to follow society's version of success can cause inertia that continues to push you along a particular, ineffective path. This path does not lead to an Authentic Success and can lead you to believe that success has an expiration date, implying that your time to succeed has come to an end. This is not true!

Now that you are further down the path and you are looking back, you see all of the obstacles you've gone through. You have experienced the biggest pandemic in a hundred years, likely the financial crisis, and, if you are old enough, you even may have gone through the S&L crisis. Many people experienced setbacks during these troubled times, and those setbacks can feel permanent. If you reflect on those experiences and filter your accomplishments through societal norms, you may get the impression that you missed your opportunity to succeed. You can feel like you have established your path and are stuck with it. You may be thinking that you have invested so much time and effort that you have to stay on this path. That is the fallacy of sunk costs, which is one of the biggest obstacles to rational decision-making. The sunk cost fallacy is the tendency to continue investing in a project because of what you've already invested in it rather than its future potential.

The news has tales of businesses pouring millions into failing products simply because of the money already spent. The logical approach would be to assess future viability and returns, but emotions often cloud judgment. Recognizing sunk costs for what they are—irretrievable investments—can free you to make decisions based on future potential, rather than past effort.

When you think, "I've already spent too much time or money to quit now," pause and reframe the situation. Ask instead, "If I were starting fresh today, would I pursue this path?" If the answer is no, it may be time to move on.

Social and traditional media can also influence your perspective on your ability to succeed. There are sensationalized posts that showcase youth success. You see it in the lists the media bombards you with. One example is the list of successful people. There are the twenty-under-twenty and the thirty-under-thirty. What about the fifty-over-fifty? If you were to listen to these lists as your sole criteria for determining whether or not you could succeed later in life, you might start believing that if you were not a success by twenty-five, your career, maybe even your chance to succeed, is over. Why is there such a focus on youth while overlooking the successes of experienced people? It is newsworthy because youth success is not a common occurrence. If a majority of young people found great success, it would not be newsworthy because it would be expected. Using these articles on youth success can give you observation bias. Have you ever thought about buying a car, only to suddenly see that many people seem to have the same one? Thinking that the car you want is popular just because you see it is not necessarily accurate. That experience is an example of observation bias.

Observation bias is a common phenomenon that skews your perception of reality through systematic errors arising when your expectations or preconceptions influence observations. Rather than objectively interpreting information, you inadvertently shape your observations to align with your existing biases. The media's showcase of youth success can skew your perspective, leading you to believe that you have missed your chance of success.

Not everyone will achieve striking success at twenty-five, thirty, or thirty-five. Everyone's life path is different. We don't all start from the same place and we don't all have the same opportunities. People also make mistakes, and many people have setbacks. Another significant factor is that you may not be ready when opportunities present themselves.

Does this mean success is out of reach? With the observation bias, you may think so. In the following chapters, I hope to help you set the record straight. We all have challenges, and we are not necessarily ready to succeed when we are young. We may have developmental issues. We may be insecure. We may have obligations that keep us from reaching our goals. Does this mean we missed the boat? Did the door close to opportunities? No! It did not! Opportunities are everywhere. They may not be the opportunities we were expecting and may not come when we expect them, but they are there if you look hard enough.

Opportunities are not all "once in a lifetime." There are opportunities all around us, and we need to go and seek them out. We need to do the work.

"Opportunity is missed by most people because it is dressed in overalls and looks like work."
–Thomas Edison

Observation bias can also impact your reflection process. People sometimes disregard their successes along the way and dwell on failures. Dwelling on failures can lead one to believe that success has an expiration date. To overcome this, make an effort to celebrate your accomplishments. As you move forward, you build your confidence and become more capable of succeeding.

Because it is flashy and garners headlines, there has always been a focus on the accomplishments of younger people. However, it seems to be more pronounced now. There is an increased emphasis on the Millennial Generation and Gen Z, which can be a source of discouragement for earlier generations. As adults, maybe even as parents or grandparents of millennials or Gen Z children, we have focused on children and given them ample opportunities to "win." The "trophies for everyone" theme has also pushed itself to the forefront in adulthood. The focus has been on young people starting businesses and succeeding. This can be seen on social media. A few clicks on a keyboard can create a company's online presence, and posting about it can make it appear successful. Posts from flailing startups can resemble those of successful companies, making it seem as though more people are achieving greater success than they actually are.

This appearance of success has perpetuated the myth that we need young people to energize our companies. Young people can do it, but they are not the only source of energy for companies. With proper preparation and focus, older people can be just as, if not more, effective in energizing companies and being great leaders. If your Authentic Success includes contributing to making a company great, there is no reason you can't. You may need to make a few changes to your approach, but you can find the success you desire.

Through my network of clients, friends, and colleagues, as well as the media, I see that people believe success has an expiration date. The people I've spoken to feel they have a certain chance, and that if they miss it, they will no longer have opportunities to succeed. This perceived lack of opportunity is a misconception and can lead people to give up on themselves. It is true that as I enter the second half of my fifties, I need to work harder to maintain my energy than I did in my twenties. I can't coast through life. I have to work to stay on top of my game.

Just because I need to work harder does not mean I cannot succeed. Through movies and maybe our parents' careers, we saw that if we work hard when we are young, then we can coast into management positions because we have "experience." If that were ever true, it is no longer true. The environment in which we work is vastly different, and we need to adapt to succeed.

Issues from this new environment include:

§   Working in flat organizations that have fewer chances to get ahead

§   Having international outsourcing that reduces the size of domestic workforces dramatically

§   Work from home programs that isolate us from our peers and superiors, so we cannot properly showcase our skills

§   Being trained for one type of career that was obsolete before we even joined the workforce

§   Falling into the trap and feeling that we can no longer get ahead if we are forty or fifty or beyond

§   Having the wrong or obsolete skill sets

§   Letting our bodies go to seed

§   Conflicting obligations

§   Having unbalanced lives

§   The fear of missing out

These are all things you can use as reasons why you should no longer try to get ahead. You'll notice I did not use the word excuse. These are not excuses. They are real, and they can affect you every day. It's best to account for them when planning your life. As you develop as an adult, you may take on responsibilities beyond your expectations. You may feel overwhelmed and trapped on a path that will prevent you from achieving the success you envisioned when you were younger. It helps to define what you mean by success. It is impossible to reach success if you don't know what success means to you. To achieve your success, it helps to consciously pursue it and be flexible in how you get there. This understanding of success is the first step in finding your Authentic Success.

Achieving an Authentic Success requires a mindset that helps you move beyond the common belief that you cannot have great accomplishments once you reach a certain age. The concept of a glass ceiling is common in the job marketplace. People who had not succeeded when they were young can even have a self-imposed glass ceiling above them.

Authentic Achiever

**A person striving to achieve
an Authentic Success**

While some people are held back, many potential Authentic Achievers tend to hold themselves back. I have seen pictures of horses standing still because they are tied to a chair. This chair is an obstacle that they could easily drag away, but they stand still. They stand still because they were tied to a similar chair when they were too small to move it. They remember the failure to move the chair, and they believe that they are tethered to a fixed object and that there is no use in trying to pull against it.

You can be affected in the same way. You may set up ceilings and walls around yourself. You may limit yourself and follow the path of least resistance, allowing yourself to be pigeonholed, staying tied to the chair. To be an Authentic Achiever, you need to take action, knocking down walls and breaking through ceilings to achieve your goals.

As many people age and take on additional responsibilities, they often become homebodies, spending less time socializing and working outside the home. People tie themselves to the chair of social/networking isolation under the guise of being too busy or helping their families. If you fall into this category, are you really too busy, or are you flopping in your favorite chair in front of the TV? You may want to measure how much time you spend in front of the TV. My guess is that you will be shocked. What better things can you do by turning the TV off? The flood of information and entertainment available today overwhelms us, and we forget that we are social creatures who thrive in the presence of others.

We also tend to mirror the actions and attributes of the people around us, so it is essential to socialize with individuals who possess character and diverse backgrounds. The adage that it is hard to fly like an eagle when you are surrounded by turkeys is true. If you can surround yourself with people who want to succeed, you will be better off. The challenge that comes with a lack of belief in an Authentic Success is that you will encounter significant resistance from others in your efforts to improve yourself, even from those who care about you.

Most people are stuck in mediocrity. Very few people will want to do the work that will turn them into an Authentic Achiever. As you seek like-minded people, you may even inspire some of your friends and family to join you on the path to becoming an Authentic Achiever. Unfortunately, you will probably find this to be the exception rather than the rule.

From the general crowd, you will hear criticism. They will "caution" you that you are too old to start a business, or that you are too fat to run a 5K race, or that forty-year-old middle managers can't make it to CEO. The funny thing is that you will hear this most often from the people who care about you. As we discussed before, these people don't want to see you get hurt, so they discourage you from taking risks. Their intentions are good, but their impact is not. If you have loved ones who want to protect you more than support you, you will need to find a more robust support system.

I have suffered this "help." I have had loved ones and friends unintentionally discourage me or make me feel like I've missed the boat. They did it to try to help me, but it only made me feel insecure and nervous. I have been told by a mentor that I was born in the wrong era. He told me that if I had started my career in the 1950s, I would have been more successful. Another person told me that I was getting a little too old to be moving forward. This friend explained how he sold his first company in his thirties. I have been told many times to take the safe way, that I have to think about my family. If I listened, you would not be reading this book. I did not cut these people out of my life. I like them. I just don't ask them for advice, and I ignore unasked-for advice.

You can also be your own worst enemy. Even if you were motivated and active when you were younger, you might have become discouraged and tired. You see people who have gotten ahead, and you see where you are, but you have forgotten how far you have come.

We all tend to measure our progress against the progress of others. We can recall from our childhood that sports and games often led to winners and losers in life, but success is not always so apparent. We all have different skills, desires, work ethic, and other factors. A person living in a studio apartment or a person living in a mansion can be a success or a failure, depending on other factors in their life. Our oversimplified perception of success, combined with the mixed messages from friends and family, can sabotage our success.

I combated this and found success using the techniques in this book. I, like you, had my share of obstacles. I learned by experience that overcoming obstacles can be fun, and making sure to listen to the right people makes the journey easier and more satisfying.

You will not be able to take away the concerns and bad advice from family members and some friends. They care about you, but they do not understand your journey. You don't necessarily want to separate yourself from your family. You need to be careful about what you share and when you share it. This way, you will get to share their company but avoid feeling the criticism.

Our heads were focused on a success that most of us could not reach by following the paths we were on. We were dispirited and confused. Many of us gave up on our goals and settled into a routine. We had the mistaken belief that we would find the perfect company and work there for our career, making steady progress up our career ladders. The flattening of organizational structures and reductions in workforces made it more challenging to move forward, and it felt like success had an expiration date.

To overcome the notion that success has an expiration date, you may need to adjust your strategy or acquire new skills. You may need to work harder. When you believe your success has expired, you can feel like you are working harder than you really are. Sometimes, a third party can give you a wake-up call and show you that you can make some changes and achieve your Authentic Success. You may need more motivation until you can build discipline.

In my experience, I see some truth in the idea that setbacks can propel people forward. However, it is not an automatic reaction. If that were the case, homeless people would be automatically propelled to becoming millionaires with no effort. Escaping the frustration energy cycle takes disciplined thought and focused action. First, to escape requires a decision to move forward. In other words, you need to hit a point that drives you to act. Second, it requires a plan to get out of your rut. Third, it requires you to execute your plan and take action. It takes focused action to get out of the rut. Nothing happens unless you take action. Finally, you need to roll with the punches and adjust your plans to reach your goals. Success is not a straight line. Remember the mountain path. Be ready to overcome obstacles as you move forward.

Frustration Energy Cycle

When you are frustrated, anxious, or depressed, you expend energy that could be used toward your goals. That energy is wasted, and you can enter a cycle of continuous energy draining, leaving you tired and unmotivated. It takes an intentional decision to break through the cycle and apply your energy to more productive endeavors.

As several boxers have insinuated, and Mike Tyson said, "Everyone has a plan until they get punched in the face." Authentic Achievers are motivated when they decide that success is not something that will happen to them, but rather something they want to achieve. It's exciting; you're making a plan and taking action. It is when you hit your first obstacle that you might have your challenge. Then, as happens in life, you encounter a second obstacle, and another, and another … Success is not a straight line. There are ups and downs. These inconsistent results can destroy motivation. That is where discipline needs to take over. Motivation is temporary. Zig Ziglar compared it to bathing and recommended doing it daily.

It is impossible to maintain motivation 100 percent of the time. You will need to step back and recharge. It is important to be intentional about recharging. Don't confuse recreation with distraction. We are constantly exposed to unfulfilling recreation. We have entertainment everywhere, 24/7, which can distract you from the work that needs to be done and delay you from achieving your goals.

These distractions can take hours of time that can be used in a more fulfilling way. We are inundated with instant gratification that distracts us from the pain and frustration we feel as we struggle. We can drown ourselves in distraction rather than setting our goals and getting to work. Even now, I realize that I have the TV on while I'm typing this chapter. I have it on mute, but why didn't I just turn it off? I am also addicted to the constant stream of entertainment. I want to distract myself from the hard work.

Our phones are bigger distractions than our televisions. It can be nearly impossible to be bored. There is a never-ending stream of content and entertainment. You can literally spend entire days looking at internet content and always have access to more.

By engaging in intentional recreation rather than mindless distraction and experiencing activities that challenge us, we can regain our energy, and we will find that we have time to exercise four days a week or more. We will find that we feel better and are not tired at 5:00 a.m. when we eat properly. By adopting a healthy lifestyle and moderating our intake of information and entertainment, we can build the energy we need to achieve our goals.

Since you have made it that far, I hope you are starting to see yourself as An Authentic Achiever. Take some time to reflect on your past performance and write down all you have achieved. When I have done it, I review my appointment calendars and notes and sometimes ask other people to help me figure out all that I have achieved. This reflection may be slow at first, but as soon as you start to build momentum, you will see that you have accomplished a great deal. You may want to start with the reflections below.

Once you see that you have had successes along the way, let's read on to see how you can achieve your Authentic Success.

Reflection

Where are you in your journey?
How do you define success?
What is holding you back?

Goals

Document what is frustrating you.

Actions

Open your mind to new ideas.

CHAPTER 2

Clearing the Path to Progress

"In the middle of difficulty lies opportunity."
—ALBERT EINSTEIN

"Resilience is accepting your new reality, even if it's less good than the one you had before. You can fight it, you can do nothing but scream about what you've lost, or you can accept that and try to put together something that's good."
—ELIZABETH EDWARDS

It is hard to own a company if you are living out of your car. It is challenging to be a good teacher if you are preoccupied with the fight you had with your spouse. It is hard to be an advocate for the homeless if you are concerned about being evicted from your home. It is not impossible to succeed, but impediments to your well-being can increase stress, making it harder to achieve authentic success. You may have to address these obstacles first.

I experienced a prolonged job search. As the sole breadwinner, I needed to provide for my family. With unemployment running out and my savings declining at an alarming rate, I could not focus on achieving my big goals. I needed to focus on one goal: to get a steady income to support my family. I put all my big goals on hold and concentrated 100 percent on getting income. During my search, I discovered new ways to earn an income, which I continued to utilize after securing a steady job. Once I had the job, I had a lot of debt that was hindering me from achieving my goals, so I put a lot of effort and resources into paying it off. Once my income was established and my debt was reduced to a manageable level, I started pursuing my big goals in earnest.

I did not give up on my goals. I performed an honest assessment of where I was in my life's journey and my ability to achieve my goals. Obstacles were preventing me from achieving those goals, so I prioritized my actions to eliminate them in order of their impact on my ability to reach my objectives. Once the obstacles were eliminated, I proceeded with a plan to achieve my Authentic Success.

Where are you in your life journey? A significant part of achievement is an honest assessment of where you are now. We all encounter challenges in life, and sometimes our life choices take us farther from our goals. This can be a difficult reflection. It is easy to fall into personal recrimination and negative self-talk. I won't tell you not to be upset by negative revelations. You can't ignore negative feelings. If you encounter these feelings, take some time to acknowledge and work through them and forgive yourself. Everyone makes mistakes, and redemption is a real possibility. Accept your failings, learn from them, and move forward.

I have made this reflection exercise a habit. My birthday is at the end of September, and I use that date as the starting point for my annual reflection. Since I made it a habit, looking back is not as difficult. It is easier because I am reviewing a shorter time period. Still, the main reason is that I have become accustomed to reviewing failures and understand the value of the lessons learned. The first time I went through this exercise was devastating for me. I looked back at decades of efforts, and at first, I only saw failures. I was very discouraged, and it wasn't until I started working with a coach that I also began to include the wins in my assessment. I find that I have achieved a lot more than I remembered. I discovered that any failures I have had (even the big ones) did not end my ability to achieve my goals. I intentionally reflect and get a true perspective on how I performed.

When completing this reflection to establish your starting line, expect to experience disappointment and negative feelings. It's natural. You would not be reading this book if you felt that you had already achieved your Authentic Success. If you find yourself in a cycle of discouragement because you are farther from your goals than you thought, consider engaging a coach, mentor, or trusted advisor to help you through it. Your past does not disqualify you from finding an Authentic Success.

It is important to know where you are when developing your plan, so you can determine whether you need extra steps to reach your goal. You may have a reputational issue (jail time, rumors, appearances of impropriety), financial issues (bankruptcy, job loss, high debt, foreclosure), family issues (divorce, childcare responsibilities), health issues (disease, fitness), or professional issues (toxic workplace, unmanageable work hours). These issues don't have to prevent you from achieving Authentic Success, but they can affect your approach, so you need a clear understanding of your current status.

Objectivity is important for this reflection. People tend to filter their perspective on their accomplishments through the societal norms they were exposed to growing up. These societal norms form a pattern that appears to establish mandatory milestones for achieving success. These norms can include attending school, earning a college degree, securing a traditional job, maintaining a diligent work ethic, and paying one's dues. Society tells you that if you do this, you will eventually find success.

When you look at this list, you may find that you have not done some of these things and feel like you don't have what it takes to succeed.

Success is not based on what you haven't achieved. It is about what you have achieved. You cannot accomplish everything due to opportunity costs, but you don't need to on your path to Authentic Success.

Opportunity Costs are an economic concept based on the costs you face from making one choice over another. Opportunity Costs are the loss of potential rewards from one course of action that results from choosing another. Choosing means that you can't experience an event that may be important to you when you need to perform a task that is vital to achieving your goals. For example, you can't go to an exercise class when you choose to go to the bar with your friends. You can't read a book when you choose to watch television. You can't go to dinner with your spouse when you choose to play softball. There are choices you must make, and those choices will impact your ability to achieve your Authentic Success. The choices listed above were not meant to be judgmental. Going to the bar can help you build relationships. That show on TV may be important. The softball game may be your exercise time. The point is to ensure that you understand that every choice comes with costs. Not all the choices are so black-and-white. You will need to reflect on your definition of an Authentic Success to make your choice.

As you start your journey to your Authentic Success, you will find out how to reinvigorate your goals and achieve success on your terms.

If you are not on a path that leads to your Authentic Success, you can actively work toward changing your path. An Authentic Success takes intentional action. If you don't make an active effort, you risk the inertia of society's expectations pushing you farther down the wrong path and away from your goals. It can be easy to succumb to this inertia and stay on the wrong path since the inertia makes it feel comfortable. It can feel like floating down a lazy river in an inner tube. The water is warm, the pace is slow; it feels like you're making progress, but you're going round and round in a loop.

The inertia gains strength when you are surrounded by people who are also following society's version of success. These people tend to provide constant reinforcement of the false belief that you have to follow society's ideals, even if it means abandoning your true goals.

I think my experience is typical of many of my peers in my generation. The popular culture of the late 1970s to the 1990s featured numerous references to the notion that success is reserved solely for the young. We ended up using movie and book characters as the models for the paths we want to follow. It showed young executives as energetic and older executives as stoic and out of touch. Movies about successful people influenced us, as did TV shows about wealthy individuals, which showcased the most attractive aspects of that life and encouraged us to desire that lifestyle. I recall an article from over thirty years ago in *Fortune Magazine* that addressed the concerns of young professionals about living on "only" $200,000 a year. This portrait of success is what we were weaned on. There was an expectation of success if we followed society's expectations.

I had all these ideas of quick success in my head. I just needed to graduate from college, and I would be on my way. I had ideas of becoming a teacher, but I was discouraged from that and encouraged to study business. I excelled in college, graduating with a double major, and had visions of a stellar career path. I had a lot of interviews at banks, and I thought I was ready to shine. Then there was the S&L crisis. One by one, the banks I had great interviews with were closed. Many, many banks went out of business, and there was a glut of real estate that flooded the market. Professional jobs were lost, many of which were never to return, and professionals had to scramble to find their place in other industries. Then there was the outflow of jobs overseas. This reduced many jobs in manufacturing. This reduction in job opportunities had an impact on the career tracks of both blue and white-collar workers. The playing field was changing, and people who were on a fixed path struggled.

Like many people, I found myself wondering what I was doing wrong. The self-doubt and anxiety reinforced that I needed to listen to society, not my ideas of success. I listened to people who lacked the expertise to guide me and others who didn't care if I achieved my goals, as long as I helped them achieve theirs. Reflect back on your experiences. You probably had similar experiences that led you to have self-doubt and anxiety.

Many people were left reeling by the dramatic economic changes. It was as if they had their ropes cut, and they were left to drift. If they did not take intentional action, they were pushed along with the tide instead of getting on a course that leads to their goals. My experience immediately after college forced me to make dramatic changes to my plans. Those changed plans led to interesting experiences and fascinating people, but it wasn't until much later that I understood that I was not focused on my Authentic Success.

Young, aggressive, but naïve people were presented as examples of success that people of my generation wanted to follow. Movies like *Wall Street* and books like *Liar's Poker* were supposed to be cautionary tales, but we turned them into anthems for the generation. Earning money at any cost was presented to us as the definition of success. The lessons taught by older, more experienced individuals in movies and books were often ignored. It was more stylish to follow the unrealistic expectations presented by pop culture and ignore the lessons of qualified mentors. This message was reflected in the courses we took in college and the careers we chose. We ended up measuring ourselves against movie and book characters. Then we started measuring ourselves against the people we knew by the standards dictated by society.

We saw people who did better than us and people who didn't make it as far, and we gauged our success by that. We did better than Joe, but Ann is doing even better than we are. We had people telling us they are proud of us for making it this far, but we still feel we haven't gone far enough. I often see this pattern in Generation X men.

How has your life experience impacted your current situation?

Everyone has a different life experience, but you can still end up unsatisfied with unfulfilled goals. By reflecting on your experience, you can identify the path changes you may need to make. This is especially important if my story above did not resonate with you. You are the author of your story. If you can understand your origins, you will be more able to craft a path that leads to your goals.

The constant state of change can give the illusion of an expiration date. Just because an era has ended does not mean that your potential for success has ended. If you are willing to adapt and change, you can find yourself with even more opportunities. When computers made typewriters obsolete, significant changes occurred that impacted people. Those who stuck with typewriting skills got left behind, but those who embraced word processing skills found new opportunities. The typist had the opportunity to adapt to the changes and to continue successfully by taking intentional action to adapt.

The process of regular career advancement has undergone significant changes and continues to evolve dramatically with advances in technology. Technology increased productivity, which reduced the need for additional workers, which in turn reduced the need for supervisors. All these factors reduced the number of traditional paths for employees to gain the experience they need to advance. When there were many leadership opportunities available, people could gain the experience they needed to achieve their goals. With the elimination of those opportunities, you need to develop your own opportunities to gain experience. You may have expected to get that experience in your twenties or thirties, but if that didn't occur, there is no reason why you can't do it now.

The structure of the organizations we worked for has changed dramatically over the last thirty years. Organizations are much flatter, with fewer opportunities for career growth and less stability. This structural change has eliminated the traditional path to career success that we were "promised" by popular culture. We found ourselves working harder for fewer opportunities. This left us vulnerable to people who would make promises for advancement if we only helped them achieve their goals. They provided opportunities and promises but failed to deliver. It can take some reflection to distinguish between career issues stemming from personal failure and those resulting from unkept promises. You should take responsibility for both issues. You own your failures, but you should also take ownership of being manipulated. By doing so, you take control and can change it, making you more likely to find your Authentic Success in the future.

The struggle to achieve career goals that don't reflect society's norms for work environment can impact your work/life balance. are. If you are working a traditional full-time job while trying to build a business or some other vocation, you may not necessarily be home at 5:30 p.m. for dinner and may not have time to do many of the things you would otherwise want to do. You also need to consider finances. Starting a business or other vocation costs money, so if you want to be able to fund your other goals, you may need to work harder and longer, which can impact the amount of time you have to spend on your new venture. An example is a stay-at-home parent. It is very hard to afford raising children without both parents working and outsourcing part of the children's care. If your goal is to have a parent stay home, you may need to give up other goals, and there's a chance that you will put a lot of stress on the working parent. It can be worth the sacrifice (my wife and I did it), but there are costs.

Another societal norm for the work environment is the two-income family. Initially, the second income helped the family get ahead. Now that income and prices have reached equilibrium, it can be difficult to make ends meet without a second income. Having one income also makes it difficult to take risks and get ahead. You never want to be caught with no income when you have a family to support, so you may avoid taking risks, which can lead to stagnation in achieving your goals. This stagnation can lead to giving up on your goals. The choice to push through the anxiety of potential lost income and the guilt of missing family events can be a hard choice to make. We can easily rationalize our giving up on our goals. There are real, valid reasons that can drive you to abandon your goals. Because of these circumstances, it is important that you confirm your definition of success, what your Authentic Success is, so you can work towards the goals you want, rather than taking the path of least resistance.

You may feel tired, frustrated, and guilty about sacrificing one activity to achieve another, only to find that your sacrifices seem meaningless due to changes in the career environment. Societal norms in the workplace can give the appearance of favoring younger people and giving the impression that success has an expiration date. The unstated message from society can appear to be that older people have had their time. They need to step aside and let go of their goals. This social norm message is that it's solely the next generation's turn to succeed because success has an expiration date is a myth. Opportunities are still available for you!

Most people do not have a direct path to success. Careers tend to meander back and forth, and goals can get put on hold for situations outside of your control. The key is to adapt to life changes as you pursue your Authentic Success. It is like hiking up a mountain road. Most people can't race straight up the mountain. To allow people to hike up the mountain, the trails are cut into the mountain in a meandering, back-and-forth pattern. Meandering can take longer to reach the top of the mountain, and it requires persistence. When the hike is challenging, many people stop at viewing areas in the middle of the mountain rather than continuing to the top; they change their goal—satisfied to see the sights from the middle of the mountain rather than persisting to see the best views at the top.

Like the people who stop at the viewing areas, you might start the negative self-talk when you find a comfortable spot on the way to your goal. You may start thinking you don't have what it takes to achieve your goal. Friends tell you how far you've come and ask if you really need to go farther. You are the only one who can answer if you have reached your Authentic Success.

Think about your career. Has it been a straight line or has it meandered? You may have started hiking up the career mountain and stopped at a less-than-ideal job. What is your next step? Do you prefer the comfort, or do you have the desire to struggle further up the mountain? You may have seen others who appear to have been helicoptered to the peak. Comparing yourself to those people can be discouraging and may lead you to want to give up. When you continue to push toward your Authentic Success, you become an Authentic Achiever. Taking action and moving forward helps you focus on your success and avoid feeling bitterness toward the people who succeed faster. Authentic Achievers do not give up; they push forward and reach their goals. Are you ready to be an Authentic Achiever?

Careers have become the social norm measure of success. Think about how you introduce yourself. When asked to give your name and tell a little about yourself, does your job come into your answer? We need to keep in mind that your career is "A" measure of success, but it is not the "THE" measure of success. You may define success differently. If you have ever experienced a sudden job loss, you know that the loss of a job can feel like a loss of part of your life. You may not have even felt like a whole person. There was something missing. Your job can be such a big part of your life that it might blind you to other opportunities. Focusing solely on your work-life as the measure of success may be an obstacle to your Authentic Success.

An extreme focus on your career may impact other goals, like wanting to be a better parent, volunteering for your favorite charity, or other things leading to your Authentic Success. Unfortunately, unless a rich relative left you a fortune or you win a huge lottery jackpot, you probably need to work to fund your life. You cannot donate money if you can't afford to feed yourself or your family. A business ethics professor from college said something that has stuck with me to this day. He said: "The business of business is to do business." He explained that a business needs to earn a profit before it can care for its employees and communities, otherwise it is just focused on survival. This concept is also applicable to individuals. It can be more difficult to work on your goals when you are struggling to put food on the table. Life requires choices. How badly do you want your goals? Do you work overtime or have a second job, which may cause you to miss other important events? These decisions, along with the realization that life requires money to live, can be daunting. You may want to follow your passions, but you need to be able to fund your life. You will likely face some difficult choices on your path to an Authentic Success.

You are human, and as mentioned earlier, you might find yourself comparing your choices and accomplishments to those of other people. If you aren't achieving at a pace you are happy with, you can get discouraged. This discouragement can lead to a lack of energy that hinders your pursuit of goals and can be exacerbated by workplace challenges. You can get into a Frustration Energy Drain Cycle in which you get tired, making work frustrating, which leads to more fatigue, ending with you feeling like you have passed your success expiration date when you are just in a rut.

If you have ever had your car slide into a rut in the road, you know that it can be a challenge to get your car out. If you haven't taken care of your car and it has bald tires or doesn't have the power it did when new, it can be even harder to get out of a rut. You might even need a tow truck to get out. A rut captures the tire and makes the tire go in a direction you may not want to go, or it keeps you stuck in one spot. It can take a lot of effort to get out.

You can personally get stuck in a similar way. If you have been in the Frustration Energy Drain Cycle for a long time, you may envision yourself at the end of your ability to succeed and lack the energy to get out of the rut yourself. You may need the support of others. This support can come from a mentor or trusted advisor, but if you don't have one and you're in a rut, it might be challenging to attract one. If people are going to mentor someone, they typically want someone with some energy and who will put some effort into the relationship. To get you out of a deep rut, you may need more than a push; you may need a tow. In this case, the "tow" can come from a career/executive coach.

The coach can provide you with techniques to help you get out of your career rut and get back on track to reaching your goals. They can also be a good sounding board. When you get frustrated, you can talk to them. By sharing your issues with someone who has no emotional attachments to you but genuinely has your best interests at heart, you will feel a burden lifted, you won't be as tired, and you will be able to continue working towards your goals. The coach can also guide you on changing your job to make it more satisfying, or if that doesn't work, to help you change companies, so you can be in an environment that will allow you to achieve your Authentic Success.

Reflection

What experiences or mistakes that you've made are holding you back?

What can you do to put those mistakes behind you?

What actions are you willing to take to move forward?

Goals

Document your plan to clear your path to progress.

Actions

Review your plan and start acting on it to prepare yourself to achieve An Authentic Success.

CHAPTER 3

You Can Be an Authentic Achiever

"It is never too late to be what you might have been."
—George Eliot

*"The time for action is now.
It's never too late to do something."*
—Antoine de Saint-Exupery

The biggest obstacle for the Authentic Achiever's success can be themselves. By not believing in yourself or by trying to succeed alone, you can put yourself at a disadvantage. Success is a team sport. It is very hard to succeed on your own. Having a support system in place can significantly improve your chances of success. This support system can include coworkers, family, and friends. This does not mean that everyone in your circle will be part of your support system. Most people will be neutral, and a few will be hostile. You can develop a support system by cultivating a few key people who can help you along. The people you invite to join you on your journey can be integral to your success. It may be cliché, but the metaphor "It is hard to fly with the eagles when you are surrounded by turkeys" is true.

In an ideal world, at work, you would be able to cultivate a network of people at different levels. You would have people more senior to you, peers, and subordinates in your support network. People more senior to you can guide you in your career and speak well of you to their peers. In return, you would help them achieve their goals by doing tasks they don't have time to do. You would identify peers with whom you can work to achieve your goals while helping them achieve theirs. Your network of subordinates would be the inverse of your network of superiors. You would support and showcase your subordinates' work, and they would help you achieve your goals by doing tasks for you. If you work in this environment, you're fortunate. With working from home and isolation that started with the pandemic, these bonds may have been broken. Work cultures have changed, making it harder to develop the relationships you need.

If you have never looked at your workplace from this perspective, don't work in an ideal workplace, or if your goals are not in line with the company's goals, it is not too late to build your team. As you work through this book, you will see that life is a team sport, and you will learn how to build your network. It is important to be selective in choosing your team members. Friends and family can be the easiest to reach out to, but they may not be the best candidates.

Your family is also a potential resource for support but can be a negative influence on you. You may also want to manage your communication with them. It is essential to communicate any changes that may affect your family. You can't just drop a bomb on your family like you are moving them to another state. However, if you are single and your extended family gets nervous about change, it might be best to drop it on them at the last minute. By controlling your communication, you can provide people with enough information to help you achieve your goals, while omitting parts that may make them nervous and discourage you from moving forward.

Working hard toward a goal so big that you cannot see the point where you accomplish it is difficult. It can be easy to get discouraged and lose faith in yourself. There are people all around you pulling you back, some who love you and want to protect you, others who want to see you fail. It might make you question whether you can make it. Being a trailblazer is hard.

Think of yourself as an explorer of old. You have just boarded your sailing vessel for a land that you believe is there, but you have no idea of the storms you will hit or if you will make it. Scary, isn't it? Sitting on your couch looks a lot safer, doesn't it? Your family doesn't want you to go because it is dangerous. There are a million reasons/excuses not to do it. Really big goals can be like that, scary. You need to have enough faith in yourself to carry through.

If you are cutting a path that no one has cut before, you don't know if you can succeed. If no one else has done it, there is a chance that it is not possible. A task can be a lot easier if you know that it has been done before. Writing a book has been that trailblazing path for me. I had written hundreds of articles over the years, but until about six years ago, I had never succeeded in writing a book. I have always had challenging jobs and sometimes very long commutes. With challenging schedules, I did not think it was possible to succeed in writing a book. My perspective of a new author was that of an underemployed writer who wrote all the time, waiting for their big break.

It wasn't until I read about Tom Clancy. He had a "real job" when he was writing, and he was able to write a book that put him on the path to greatness in the writing world. If you don't know if someone has accomplished a task, it is the same as believing no one has done it. If you do not believe it can be done, it can feel nearly impossible for you to do it. The adage "If you think you can or can't, you are right" is true. It is all up to you.

Even if you are doing something that no one else in the world has ever succeeded at, you can find examples to follow. If you are an inventor, Edison's overcoming of failure in creating the light bulb is inspiring. If you are a politician or an aspiring leader, Abraham Lincoln's life will help you. If you are a teacher, reading about Helen Keller can inspire you to try harder with students who are struggling academically.

You can have all the inspiration in the world, but it may still not be enough. There can still be the nagging sensation that you may have missed the boat, that you are too old, or you should just go gently into that good night. It helps to have examples of people who succeeded later in life. Thankfully, there are a lot of them. Hopefully, you can find one in your network. Having a living, breathing person you can talk to is a real shot in the arm when it comes to being inspired. If you don't have a person like that in your network, there are a lot of famous people who are Authentic Achievers. Here is a brief list. Find the person who inspires you. Read about that person. If you are a visual person, hang their picture on your wall. Stay inspired. Use the trail they blazed to make your journey easier.

- § **Stan Lee** was in his forties when he reinvented Marvel Comics
- § **Mary Kay Ash** was forty-five years old when she started her cosmetics company
- § **Rodney Dangerfield** didn't find success in comedy until he was nearly fifty
- § **Julia Child** started to learn about French cooking at thirty-two and opened a cooking school at forty
- § **Ray Kroc** was in his fifties when he found success with McDonald's
- § **Laura Ingalls Wilder** published her first book at age sixty-five
- § **Harland Sanders** was in his sixties when he founded Kentucky Fried Chicken
- § **Anna Mary Robertson Moses** (Grandma Moses) started painting in earnest when she was seventy-eight years old.

There are many individuals beyond those on the list who have achieved success later in life. You can find the one that inspires you.

Theodore Roosevelt inspires me. He was sickly as a child, but made a conscious effort to get himself into shape to be able to live the life he wanted to live. I find his life inspirational, and I want to emulate parts of it. I say 'parts of it' because there are things he did that don't fit my values. I am mentioning it to show that a person does not need to be perfect to inspire you. There may only be one segment of the person's life that inspires you. The key is to find an example of success that you can relate to and use to help you blaze your trail. You may be doing something no one else has done before, but there is someone out there who has accomplished something that can inspire you on your journey. Let their story help you blaze the trail. Learn from their experiences. There is no reason to reinvent the wheel.

The key is to emulate the traits we admire, not copy the actions of the inspirational person. You are your own person, not a copy of someone else. Seek out your own unique path, while emulating others. You have probably heard that we can fake it until we make it. There have been times in my career when I had no idea how to execute the tasks I was assigned. Because I had demonstrated an ability to get things done, I was assigned more challenging and foreign tasks. To keep going, I needed to fake it until I made it. I kept calm, stayed inspired, and learned the things I needed to learn to get the job done as I was doing the job.

Society tells us to be strong, independent people. Many people translate independent into alone, working on their own, not listening to anyone, and just doing it their way. Walking the path alone puts you at a disadvantage since you only have your experience to leverage. There is a story of a man who gave up everything during the gold rush to be a gold miner. He bought a plot of land, and he started digging. He actually found some gold and sold the ore for enough money to buy mining equipment. He was going strong until the vein of gold ended.

He searched and searched but could not find more gold. Discouraged, he sold the mine and equipment for a fraction of what he paid, and he went home. The individual who purchased it hired a geologist and discovered a vein of gold three feet from where the first person had stopped, which turned out to be a very productive mine.

This story is usually told as a tale of perseverance. If the first person stuck with it, he would have gotten the gold. To me, it is more of a story about learning from others. The first man went out on his own and lacked all the necessary expertise. The second man also lacked expertise, but he acquired it by hiring an expert. He learned from others. We need to be open to help from others. It helps to set aside your ego and learn from others, leverage their experience rather than learning through trial and error on your own. Leveraging other people's expertise helps you leapfrog the process. You are not in school. It is okay to copy from another person's homework. Learn from their successes and failures and apply those lessons to your life.

When you are working on something you haven't done before, you might find yourself getting stuck. Sometimes, we need an objective third party to provide guidance. The people around us and who care about us have expectations and biases. When you work with or live with people, they get certain expectations of you. They expect you to do certain things, act a certain way, and that leads them to picture you in a certain position. Those expectations can lead to being pigeonholed. If your boss sees you as a worker bee, he may not groom you to be a leader. If your kids see you as standoffish, they may not trust you enough to share their problems with you. If you drink a lot when you are with your buddies, they may not see you as a potential triathlete. Our inner circle may have expectations of us that could hinder them from being effective advisors for any life changes we want to make.

The potentially prejudiced advice from your inner circle can be avoided by hiring a coach. Whether you are looking to get into shape or get ahead at work, a coach is a useful asset. A coach possesses expertise in helping individuals achieve their goals. They can teach skills but can also serve as a sounding board and provide customized advice for specific situations. Over time, they get to know you, so they can provide you with personalized service without the level of bias that your inner circle may have.

When you engage with a coach, it is important that they are qualified. Most people lack the skills necessary to lead and coach others effectively. Even if your boss wants to help you grow, they probably don't have the skills necessary to accomplish it, and it can do more harm than good. One of my first manager's first coaching sessions with me addressed the importance of scheduling lunch every day, not to meet people, just to eat. These days, it is unlikely to find a boss willing to help, as they may fear the appearance of favoritism. Many companies also have misguided rules that keep managers from coaching their people.

This means that there are limited opportunities for coaching in the workplace, and many of those opportunities will be executed poorly. That leaves the only option of a third-party independent coach who wouldn't be afraid to look at you objectively, help you assess your strengths and weaknesses, and have the expertise to guide you forward. Each of our paths is unique. Having a person who can give you customized guidance based on your needs can help you get ahead a lot faster than you would be able to on your own.

When looking for a coach, consider your goals and starting point. Coaches can be general or specific. As you are starting out, you probably want a general coach, someone who can help you develop your plan and get you started on your path to an Authentic Success. As you progress on your journey, you will find weaknesses that you will want to overcome, so you may need specialized coaches.

I have leveraged coaches for many years. I have a general executive coach, but I also have specific coaches to help me develop specific skills.

I have a speaking coach to help me be a better speaker, but also to help me build a speaking business. I have a book-writing coach who helps me not only with my book but also with making it more marketable. I have a fitness trainer to show me how to develop a workout plan. I have had other coaches along the way. The coaching relationship is not permanent. Once you overcome your obstacle, you may no longer need that coach. I am confident that once you have a coach, you will maintain coaching relationships throughout your life.

What can coaching do for you? Let's say you are a middle manager who is tired of the corporate rat race and wants to start a business. You have always wanted to open a breakfast shop. You have the goal of opening a breakfast shop, and you know where you are now: middle management. How do you make the jump? We all hear that a high percentage of businesses fail each year. Does that mean you shouldn't pursue your goals? No, it means you should have a good idea of what you're getting into and have a plan to get there. Does being a middle manager give you all the skills you need to be a breakfast shop owner? Probably not, when you are a business owner, you are responsible for everything; as a middle manager, you are responsible for your little section of the world, and you are also not preparing food and drinks for customers.

A coach specializing in entrepreneurship and the restaurant industry is someone you want to meet. Flipping through the channels on your television, you will see shows about people going in to help fix restaurants, bars, and hotels. Although the shows can be overly dramatic, they effectively demonstrate how coaching can be helpful. The coach gives you advice on things you probably haven't thought of. They can also help you with your transition plan. There may even be ways to start your business while you are still working, so you can have the benefit of your income while you are getting your business off the ground. They can help you avoid the pitfalls.

The same goes for someone who wants to stay in corporate America. If you are stuck in the doldrums of middle management, an executive coach can help you plan your path to C-suite positions. They can identify your failings and help you make corrections. Due to the biases and expectations mentioned earlier in the book, you may need to leave your current company to start fresh. A coach can give you objective guidance on how to proceed.

Coaches can help with things other than careers. Success goes beyond work. Hobbies, families, religious beliefs, and other avocations also add to a successful lifestyle. If you are overworked, you may want to go to a life balance coach. If you lack confidence, consider coaching to help you develop the confidence you need.

The people you spend time with can have a material impact on how much success you can achieve. If you hang out with negative people, they can negatively impact your attitude. That does not mean that you get rid of friends. You can compensate for a negative influence by managing how you communicate with and how much time you spend with certain people. As you grow as a person, you may find that you have friends only because they are easy to hang out with but are hurting you more than helping you. You may find new friends who are more aligned with your interests. These people can help you achieve your goals.

When you have spent time neglecting your Authentic Success to help others with their goals, it is easy to feel down on yourself and give up on your goals. It is very hard to succeed when you are in the Frustration Energy Cycle and feeling tired, frustrated, embarrassed, and hopeless. However, that state of mind can act as a slingshot to success when you get out of your slump. Changing your perspective from "You're too late to succeed" to "You've hit a setback" can make a big difference. Motivational resources use the analogy of a bow pulling back an arrow. You can't shoot an arrow without pulling back the string on the bow. If you experience a setback, it can act as a bow pulled back, propelling you forward.

**"We become what we think about most of the time, and that's the strangest secret."
–Earl Nightingale**

An example that demonstrates the impact of the Frustration Energy Cycle is a prolonged job search. When you are out of work and are not getting the results you want, it is easy to fall into the Frustration Energy Cycle and feel like you are no longer able to succeed. You get tired of looking so hard. You are frustrated by the lack of jobs. You then get a feeling of hopelessness and embarrassment that you are no longer able to find a job, and your best days are behind you. When one gets to this point, one has reached the point of decision. Do you give up, believe that success has an expiration date and settle for whatever life serves you, or do you move forward on the seemingly impossible path to your Authentic Success?

Discipline helps you through the tough spots. You know what you should do, and it's easier when you're excited and motivated. If you build a structure for action when you are motivated, you have something to follow when your motivation wanes. If you have built discipline into your structure, you can maintain the drive to keep going. As you continue, you develop habits that foster inertia and propel you forward toward success. Inertia works both ways. We talked earlier about how the power of inertia can hold you back. If used properly, it can also propel you forward. The inertia can be like the motorized walkways in airports. You move along, even if you're too tired to walk. For example, when you build the habit of getting up early for a period of time, you find yourself getting up before the alarm goes off. The more you work out, the more you miss it when you can't. By developing productive habits, you will find it easier to achieve your goals.

As you have probably realized, getting out of the Frustration Energy Cycle takes intentional effort. It is not the easiest path to take. If you don't make an intentional effort to stay on the path, you can fall into the path of least resistance. The path of least resistance is the easiest path to take. Most of the time, that path does not lead to success. At best, it yields the same results you are currently achieving. At worst, you can slide farther from achieving your goals. If you are overweight, the path you are on probably consists of unhealthy eating and a sedentary lifestyle, rather than healthy eating and exercise. If you are in a job rut, the path is to keep doing what you are doing and hoping things will get better. If you have poor communication with your spouse, the path is often being defensive, rather than being empathetic and open to understanding. Just like people walking in the same direction carve a path in the grass, your habits carve a path in your life. Habits, whether positive or negative, drive the direction of your path, which can be toward your goals or away from them. It is up to you. Habits can lead to excellence or mediocrity.

People usually focus on bad habits because advertisements bombard us with advice on how to beat them. Smoking, overeating, sedentary lifestyle, etc., are thrown at us as things we need to change. What is the one thing all of these commercials have in common? They all say that their products will make the change easy, but in truth, it is very difficult. Once you acknowledge that this path is hard, develop a plan, and act while you are motivated, you can establish positive habits that will help you push through obstacles and achieve your goals. Push through the ruts until you build these actions into a positive habit.

To make any change is hard. Even when a baby has a dirty diaper, they cry when you change them into a new one. Sitting with a dirty diaper, although uncomfortable and unhealthy, is easier than going through the diaper change. We often share similar impulses to resist change as adults. Being in a job that holds you back, or being in an abusive relationship, or being on an unhealthy lifestyle becomes the new normal, a comfort zone. Like the baby with the diaper change, we resist any change even if we know we would be better off making it. The benefit of establishing a good habit is that once you establish a habit, you build inertia, which makes the habit harder to break, so you can use it to your advantage.

Motivation ebbs and flows. Nobody can be motivated 100 percent of the time. Once the motivation is gone, if you have not built the discipline, you will fall back into the Frustration Energy Cycle. The process of building your Authentic Success starts with motivation, continues through discipline, and then brings you over the finish line through established habits. The process leads you to develop positive habits that you won't want to abandon. I can't repeat it enough. An Authentic Success is not a straight path. It is not even a single path. It is a meandering forest trail with obstacles. You may not always be able to see the end of the path. You may not have all the necessary tools when you begin the path. It can be both scary and grueling, yet also rewarding and exciting. Your discipline will help you stick with it during the scary and grueling times. One of the most insidious obstacles you will encounter is critics who will tell you habit changes don't work. They will say that people gain the weight back, they start smoking again, or they are back sitting in front of the TV. Having the support group mentioned earlier can help you drown out the critics and stay on track.

It can be hard to find a model to follow. An Authentic Success means different things to different people, and An Authentic Success needs to be balanced. Would you consider a wealthy man who has alienated his family and is now alone to be successful? Would you consider someone who worked really hard but neglected their health and ultimately developed preventable health problems to be successful? Being focused on a goal in isolation from your other life needs can help you achieve that goal, but it does not necessarily lead to Authentic Success. You need to define what Your Authentic Success is.

§   Does it mean you want to own a company?

§   Does it mean you want to be a great teacher or a great parent?

§   Do you want to be an advocate for the homeless or against animal cruelty?

To have an Authentic Success plan it helps to have ancillary goals to support your main goal. An example is wanting to hold a senior management position. To get it while achieving an Authentic Success, the Authentic Achiever needs to work on other goals, such as

1. Having the energy to work the required hours. To do that, they need to have:

    a. fitness goals

    b. diet goals

2. Having a happy home. To have that, they need to:

    a. live within their means to avoid financial stress

    b. spend time and talk with their family to make sure they are an engaged participant

    c. be as good a provider as they can be as they reach their goals

Just because you plan for an Authentic Success does not mean that you will always have a balanced life. I took risks that left me with significant financial stress. There were times when I was working so hard that I lost touch with my family. There were times when I forgot my fitness and became very overweight. You may lose focus on one goal or another as you pursue an Authentic Success. Don't get discouraged. Take a step back, reflect on what happened, and get back on the path.

By pushing your limits, you open yourself up to failure. Failures are part of the mountain path to An Authentic Success. Failure is intimidating to many people. The fear of failure can better be described as the fear of being ridiculed by your peers. This fear of ridicule can push people to stay in their comfort zone and avoid taking action to achieve Authentic Success. If you want to open a business and people are telling you how risky it is, you may not go for it. Not because it is too risky, but because you are afraid of what people will say if you fail. There is a good chance that those people are not experts and may have only heard about risks on TV.

When you are being influenced by the people around you, remember that you have information that the others don't. You know what you are capable of, what you are willing to sacrifice, and how hard you are willing to work. When developing your support system, take counsel from people with experience who have your interests at heart. It's best to have honest, experienced advice. An experienced coach will give you the guidance you need to achieve your goals, unlike an inexperienced advice giver, who may discourage you from reaching your full potential.

You will be amazed at how many "experts" come out of the woodwork when you start talking about doing something different. In my martial arts experience, I have heard many people refer to other styles as watered-down or ineffective. These people have never been trained in these styles. They were just listening to the marketing pitch their kids' teacher used to keep the kids in their school. By listening to these "experts", people missed out on having a good teacher with an effective style.

By listening to people who are the most experienced, not the loudest, you will get the information you need to achieve An Authentic Success. Caution is required because many people want to feel important, so they exaggerate their experience to make themselves feel significant. You need advice that will help you, not pump up the ego of one of your peers. Choose your counselors wisely. Look for experience over enthusiasm when building your support network.

It is important to set your own path and not compare your pace of success with your peers. People don't all develop a solid experience base at the same rate. There are a few people who graduate from high school or college and are ready to start a business or run a company, but they are the exception, not the rule. It is not even that common. The fact that it is unusual is what makes those achievers newsworthy. If a high level of youth success were the norm, it would not make the news. Great success in life requires experience, and people acquire it in various ways and at different rates. Envying other people's experiences is not a valuable use of time. It is usually best to cherish your past experiences and use them to propel you forward.

My high school experience is a good example. The high school I went to borders a struggling city and a well-off suburb. There were students with wealthy parents and students with struggling parents who did not want their kids to go to an inner-city school. The students were in the same environment. They had the same opportunities presented to them, but they lacked the same ability to take advantage of them. Some students were unable to afford certain opportunities. Some students were distracted by things happening in their neighborhood. Some students had parents who did not have English as a first language. Although the students were all presented with the same opportunities, their ability to take advantage of them varied. It is a lazy analysis to conclude that disadvantages lead to less significant experiences. People can learn determination and persistence from disadvantages, and people can feel entitled when presented with advantages. It is how one uses their experiences that counts.

Some people are not mature enough when they start adulthood. Maybe they fooled around and may not have known the opportunities presented to them, or they had talents that were not applicable at the time, or talents that had yet to blossom. Schools tend to put people with these factors into the same box as people who are more mature or may have a more conventional talent pattern. It can be easier for teachers to leave people with less conventional or yet-to-be-discovered talents behind and focus on the "in the box" students.

Out-of-the-box students may not experience the same level of success as their more mainstream peers and can be discouraged to the point of not pursuing the talents they possess. Those students could be left behind on the success train when they are younger, which can create a pattern of failure in life that they would need to overcome with proper guidance and motivation. I have seen great teachers who motivate out-of-the-box kids, but not every teacher has that talent. The people who guide you in life can significantly impact how you use your experiences to succeed.

Additionally, some individuals may have developmental issues. They may struggle with reading or math, or social skills. Often, these students are segregated even within their own class. This segregation can get these students labeled as stupid or weird, making it more difficult for them to integrate into the class as they overcome their difficulties.

School systems have budgets, and schools need to teach as many children as possible, so there is a focus on core skills that use testing to measure success. This testing regime can leave many marginalized students behind. They are often labeled as failures for not succeeding at tasks that most people never encounter in the working world. People often forget that most individuals don't use calculus or even algebra on a daily basis, so a student's difficulty in math doesn't necessarily mean they are prevented from succeeding.

Early success and academic achievement do not necessarily equate to success in life, but early failure in school or career can put people on a path that leads to future failure. Early success is something to be celebrated. People work hard and deserve to be recognized for their achievements. The problem comes when we compare our experiences with others without an objective eye on what each of us was ready for. If you are not number one in your class and believe that only the number one student succeeds, you may get the mistaken idea that you cannot succeed. When we look at it objectively, we might find a lesson.

Lesson 1: Potential

You could have gotten to number one if you had worked harder. Now you know that you need to put in more effort.

Lesson 2: Persistence

You don't have certain skills to be the number one student. I know people who struggled with math in high school but took basic classes at community college that helped them catch up and learn. It is never too late to learn.

Lesson 3: Adaptability

You don't necessarily need the societal norm skills like anatomy or calculus to succeed. You have unique skills you can offer.

Bucking societal norms is hard and can feel isolating. It is important to have a support system, but we need to choose the right one. Your friends and family are the people closest to you, but they may not necessarily be the best choices for your support system. Friends and family try to protect us and encourage us to do better, but they can end up perpetuating the myths that early success is the only success or that staying in safe spaces is the prudent place to be. People who care about you want to protect you from getting hurt, so they caution you against anything they see as having the potential of causing you pain. They do not consider the chances of gain to be much higher than those of getting hurt. They might caution you not to take risks or see what they consider to be your past failures and project failure into your future, even though you learned great lessons from the situations that societal norms might categorize as failures.

"The number one reason people fail in life is because they listen to their friends, family, and neighbors." –Napoleon Hill

A protective tendency starts with parents protecting children from dangers. From infancy with child-proofing the house, to requiring a helmet when riding a bike, to establishing a curfew when starting to drive a car. This protective tendency from family and friends can follow you into adulthood, with your loved ones advising you that it is too risky to pursue a new job, move to a new city, or start your own business. In the spirit of protecting you from dangers, they end up giving bad advice and limiting your progress. They can hinder you even though they are trying to help you.

Unfortunately, there are times, however, when people are trying to hurt you. There are abusive relationships that leave people feeling stupid and unworthy of success. This relationship does not make a person a failure, but it can plant a seed in their minds that puts them on the path to failure, making it more challenging for them to get back on the path to success. These situations can take time to overcome, and as a result, you may miss out on opportunities and the "fast track" to success. When people experience setbacks like this, it is important to reassess their attitude and mindset, so they don't get discouraged while learning to succeed at their own pace.

Physical and mental flexibility are crucial in being an Authentic Achiever. Circumstances are constantly changing, and you need to be able to take advantage of those changes without being overwhelmed by them. Whether it's technological or economic changes, you need to stay on top of new challenges of all kinds. A belief that "that's the way we always did it" is just as limiting as an attitude that success has passed you by. Both are static attitudes. Remaining static in a dynamic environment is like being an abandoned shed in a tornado. You will either be worn down or carried away by the circumstances around you. You will not get the desired results by doing what you have always done. Adapting to a new environment helps you achieve your Authentic Success.

If you are going to make it to the next level, you need to change your game. An Authentic Success is just that. You are changing and opening yourself to new opportunities. You are pragmatic enough to change what you are doing, to change your goals, and to reach your goals. It can be more challenging when you are older. You may feel like you have been beating your head against the wall for years and years, and you may be tired. You may want to rest and give up.

To exacerbate the situation, as we age, our bodies change. If you are overweight and stiff, it can be challenging to get around. You may experience less energy, which can alter your perspective. From my experience, being heavy also changes the way people look at you. People may tend to discount what you have to say. It helps to stay in shape and eat right so you can make it through the late nights and hard work that comes with success. Fitness gives you mojo, and you feel more powerful when you are fit and flexible. Remember, fitness does not mean becoming a fitness model. You don't have to be a bodybuilder or a marathon runner. Being able to tie your shoes without having to sit down can be more useful than bench-pressing 300 pounds.

In everyday life, flexibility can be more important than strength. We are more likely to have to bend down and pick something up than we are to have to move a heavy object. Flexibility helps us get into small cars and other tight spaces. When I was heavier, I had to hide my trouble getting out of a particularly small Uber. It was apparent I was having trouble, and even more evident that I was trying to hide it. Situations like that can be embarrassing. No one will bat an eye at you if you can't lift a heavy object, but having trouble getting out of a car is a different matter.

Understanding how your body responds to situations is also important. If you don't bounce back from long workdays, nights out, or workouts as easily as you used to, you may want to plan your days and manage your diet and activity to allow you to keep pace. My firsthand experience includes working out with strength training and having trouble getting out of bed the next morning. My long commute exacerbated this fatigue. After being in the car for one and a half hours, I needed to take my time getting out of the car, and I felt old. My mobility improved when I worked on my flexibility, and I felt younger. To get there, I combine a mixture of strength and flexibility, allowing me to feel younger and have the energy to keep pushing. You may want to experiment to see what works best for you. Just like your definition of success is different from mine. What makes you feel better about yourself can be different from what it was for me.

Many people have been programmed since they were toddlers on how to see success. The need for early success and instant gratification is reinforced from a young age. Sports are a good example. Sports teams and preparation camps often start when kids are very young, and those teams can be highly competitive. There is the pressure that if the young kids don't participate in these teams and camps, they won't succeed when they are older.

When driving around town parks, we see the little kids at T-ball and in their football uniforms. I even saw a video online of kids' strength training. The pressure to succeed at a very young age can be overwhelming. My son is an example. He decided that he wanted to wrestle in high school. When he started, he found he was playing catch-up. Many of his teammates had been wrestling for years. Discovering that you are far behind your peers can be a point at which many people become discouraged. They realize they are behind and quit. My son followed a different path and continued through, having a relatively successful run. Now that high school is over, many of the experienced kids quit, but my son has persevered with the fighting arts, transitioning into Brazilian Jiu-Jitsu and Judo. He saw what he wanted and went for it. He was an Authentic Achiever in competitive wrestling, even as a high schooler. When you are in your forties and see a gap between where you expected to be and where you are, it can be even more discouraging and seem like an even bigger obstacle to getting back on track.

As an Authentic Achiever, your choices drive you. Kids and even young adults can be more driven by their surroundings. Their friends and family influence them, and their circumstances as they experience that change. As Authentic Achievers, we need to internalize motivation as we start to see new opportunities. We need to be cautious as we make decisions without the guidance we had as children; there can be a tendency to follow the path of least resistance, which often leads to deciding on doing nothing. When you do nothing, you can miss opportunities and fall into the influence trap. When you are not intentionally driving your life, you may find yourself acting on the whims of other people. Like a boat without a rudder, the tide will push you in the direction that other people dictate. You can end up helping other people achieve their goals while doing nothing to achieve your own goals. When you are on a path that pursues other people's goals at the expense of your own, you may be unable to leave it immediately. You may need to take incremental steps to get on the path that leads to your goals. If you work in a traditional work setting with a boss and a fixed set of tasks, you may have limited choices for growth in that specific environment. You may need to overcome some obstacles before you can get on a path that leads to your goals. Addressing those obstacles can mean making some choices on how we treat ourselves, including how active we are. Working in a sedentary environment can drain our energy and leave us feeling lethargic. When you feel lethargic, you may not be motivated to put in the effort required to make the necessary changes and set yourself on a successful path.

It is helpful to have a group around you for support and to act as a sounding board. This group does not need a formal support group. This group can be a bunch of friends or a networking group. Success-oriented people are all around you, and you need to find them. Even though it can be informal, it is not optional. You have and will continue to act like the people around you, so you need to surround yourself with people you want to emulate.

Not all of the people who discourage you are doing it with your best interests at heart. Some people will try to hold you back to make themselves feel better. You are not the only one feeling tired and lost. There is a whole group of people who feel that way. They are the gigantic mass of people in the middle who have gotten somewhere, but not necessarily to the place they wanted to go. They have moved past the beginning, but they have not reached the destination they expected. They are stuck in the middle. They work hard, but they don't have a plan; they want to succeed, but they're unwilling to put in the necessary work. They have experienced setbacks, and those setbacks have discouraged them. They believe they are destined to be stuck in the middle and dislike the idea of people breaking free from the middle. You don't want to be influenced by their behaviors or take the advice that keeps you stuck in the middle with them, not failures, but also not successes.

"A successful man is one who can lay a firm foundation with the bricks others have thrown at him."
–David Brinkley

When you start to push yourself to achieve your goals, some of the people around you will ridicule your efforts to break free from the masses in the middle and reach your potential. These people perpetuate the myth that if you do not succeed by a certain age, you are out of opportunities. This mass of people causes inertia that holds others back. They can pull on you like deep mud pulling on your feet as you are walking through a swamp. They do not want you to succeed; they want you to be stuck with them in shared mediocrity. If you succeed, it shows that success is achievable, even if the people around you have not done it. They would rather believe that success is not possible.

You should disregard these individuals and, whenever possible, steer clear of them. There are enough obstacles to reaching challenging goals. You don't need to add additional barriers and traps by associating with people who want you to stay in the middle, or worse, people who want to see you fail. You need to insulate yourself from people who will hold you back or push you down. You will need to make an effort to find individuals who are willing to succeed. Most people are in the gigantic middle and don't believe that people can succeed after a certain age.

It is decision time. Do you want to be an Authentic Achiever or stay on the path of least resistance? Becoming an Authentic Achiever starts with a decision to succeed. Now the work begins. You must adjust your environment to be more receptive to your success. You have chosen the people with whom you want to associate. You need to focus on yourself. If you do not work on yourself, you will not get to the places you want to go. Lastly, you need to prepare yourself for success, intellectually and physically.

Looking back, I have taken risks, and some did not pay off. Some of them put me in financial straits. I was unable to take my family on vacations or live in a large house, but we managed to get by. I put in long hours even now, but I found ways to spend time with my family. I've balanced my life, so I've generally been successful, even when I've faced career setbacks. The key is to keep pushing, getting the right information, and moving forward.

I wrote this book not just for you, the reader, but also for me. The path of an Authentic Success is not an easy one, and we all need reminders to keep us on track. While this book will help you prepare for the next step, it is also helping me stay on track. Success is a journey as well as a destination. The rest of this book will give you ideas on how to set yourself up for success, no matter where you find yourself at this point in your life. Being an Authentic Success is not an easy path, and it will be harder for some than it is for others, but it can be very satisfying.

It's time to start your journey. Each chapter will give you ideas on how to move forward, and as you reach the end, you will find techniques to bring it all together. As you read the book, you will have the opportunity to reflect, Set Goals, and Develop Action plans. I recommend that you get a notebook to track your reflections and document your goals and action plans.

By reading the first section, you have taken the first step. You have greatness within you. I hope this book helps you discover it and achieve the success you've only dreamt about.

Reflection

Who inspires you to succeed?
Who supports you and who hinders you in achieving your goals?
What is holding you back?

Goals

Document what you need to accomplish to get on a path to your Authentic Success.

Actions

Get a notebook to document your ideas.

Develop Your
Success Toolbox

CHAPTER 4

The Turbocharged Mindset

*"We are what we repeatedly do.
Excellence, then, is not an act, but a habit.*
–Will Durant

*"If you are not willing to risk the usual,
you will have to settle for the ordinary."*
–Jim Rohn

As you evolve as a person, you gain experience. This experience can be a two-edged sword. The first edge is the knowledge that will help you move forward. The second edge is the inertia of living life the way you've always done it. The first edge will help drive you forward. The second edge may have served you in the past, but it can hold you back in the future. The inertia from the second edge is caused by things like:

§ The obsolete habits developed over time

§ Prejudices against new things

§ Fear of new technology

§ Arrogance from past successes

Inertia is neither inherently good nor inherently bad. It is a force that either brings you closer to your goals or farther away from them. My wife and I were at the airport and took one of the moving walkways to get to our gate. The walkways are faster than regular walking, making them useful tools. We were talking and missed the fact that we were approaching our gate and ended up going past it. The same tool that could have taken us to our goal faster, took us farther from our goal when we used it improperly. The same principle works with your goals. If, from your experience, you have developed a fitness habit, you don't want to drop it because you have built inertia. However, if you have made a habit of going to a networking group from which you have never gotten a lead, you might want to reconsider that habit.

It is not always easy to determine which experiences will help guide you forward and which ones will hold you back. It can be easier to just accept inertia and continue doing what you're doing, staying on the path of least resistance. Going down the path of least resistance can seem like making progress, but if it doesn't bring you closer to your goals, then it's not a productive use of your time.

You may be asking, "Is experience good or bad?" It's neither. Experience is one of the tools in your toolbox. Its value depends on how you use it, and how you use your experience has a lot to do with your mindset.

If you have a stagnant mindset that keeps you focused on the past and limits your adaptability in the future, you may find that your experience is working against you. And you are setting yourself up for the Frustration Energy Cycle. If you keep doing what you are doing, you keep getting what you've been getting. If you want to achieve more, you need to leverage your knowledge, overcome inertia, and embrace change.

You may have heard the quote, if you keep doing what you're doing, you'll keep getting what you're getting. In a dynamic environment, that is the best-case scenario. In a dynamic environment, if you keep doing what you're doing, you will start getting less and less over time. A stagnant mindset leads to obsolescence and diminishing returns.

However, with the right mindset, you will find that the busier you become, the more you accomplish. When you leverage your mindset, you become more efficient with your time, even when you're busy. People tend to let the timelines for jobs stretch to the time they have. If you set aside a Saturday to clean the garage, it tends to take up the entire day. If, however, something comes up where you must do something else in the afternoon, you'll find you can get the same task done in just the morning.

Think back to a time when you had to complete a task by a deadline in order to do something you wanted to do. Maybe it was finishing a project so that you could go on vacation. I bet you found the time and energy to finish the project so that you could go on vacation. With the right mindset, you can find the time and energy to accomplish tasks more efficiently.

You can use this mindset to your advantage. If you schedule more tasks, you will find you get more done. Once you develop your mindset, you will improve your time management efficiency. This means that if you schedule goal-related tasks, you will find that you can complete your other tasks without any harm. You may have found "more time" by being busy. Being busy is a key to avoiding the Frustration Energy Cycle. Effective, focused activity can eliminate frustration. An efficient mindset enables you to tap into your full potential and achieve authentic success.

"Rarely have I seen a situation where doing less than the other guy is a good strategy."
–Jimmy Spithill

We all have different talents and skills. Olympic runners are successful. Does that mean we are not successful runners if we do not run that fast? No, we must measure against our own goals. If we are capable of and have the goal of running a 5K road race in under thirty minutes, and we do not train, and we miss our goal, we are not successful. On the other hand, if we don't train and we do hit the goal, the goal is too low, so we are not meeting our full potential as an Authentic Success.

You can hit goals and still be stuck in mediocrity. If your goal is to be less than fifteen minutes late for work every day, and you are only five minutes late, you have hit your goal, but it does not help you escape mediocrity. You need to have challenging, meaningful goals that move you in the direction you want to go. Once you have set those goals, you are on your way to escaping mediocrity.

It is important to have the right mindset when you are setting your goals. Setting big goals can be scary, so if you do not have the right mindset, you may set your goals too low. You may see failure around every corner, and most people hate and fear failure. You may put up walls in your mind, such as "no time", "wrong skills", or "obligations", so we don't think we can achieve big goals. People tend to create obstacles in their minds, including limited time, lack of skills, or misaligned priorities. If we think something will take a long time and obsess over it, we may find ourselves spending more time thinking about the task than getting other things done.

If you schedule your time around what you want to accomplish, you can achieve it. It is similar to the experiment on whether a jar is filled. In this experiment, a teacher fills a jar with rocks and asks the students if the jar is filled. They say yes. The teacher then pours gravel into the jar around the rocks and asks if it is full. When the students say yes, the teacher pours sand around the gravel, and the students are a little less sure that it is full. Finally, to complete the example, the teacher poured water over the sand. That fills the jar. Like that jar, our day has a lot more space than we think it does.

The way we fill our days has similarities with the jar in the order in which we put things in it. If we fill the jar with sand first (the least important tasks), we will not be able to fit all the rocks in. The same goes for our days. If we fill our days with the little tasks, we will not have room for the big tasks. If we spend our Saturday morning posting memes on Facebook, we won't have time to clean the garage. However, if we clean the garage first, we'll find that we have time to go on Facebook before heading out in the afternoon. Prioritize your day, and you will find you get a lot more done without sacrificing your other tasks. You can also utilize automation and delegation to maximize your time. If you clean the garage, you have only cleaned the garage. If you first put clothes in the washer, dishes in the dishwasher, and ask the kid down the street to mow the lawn, and then clean the garage, you will have clean clothes, clean dishes, a mowed lawn, and a clean garage.

Changing your mindset to one of achievement can help you increase your productivity, allowing you to accomplish more and lead a more satisfying life. This mindset can open your mind to using more tools and delegating some tasks, allowing you to accomplish more.

There is value in delegation, and you can accomplish more, as illustrated in the example above. Delegation does not have to be to a person. You can use technology to enhance your productivity. When you prioritize your day, consider which tasks are best suited for outsourcing or delegation. To maximize my time, I delegate tasks to others and utilize technology to enhance my productivity. I also outsource. I send my dress shirts out to be cleaned and ironed. Delegation leaves me more time to work on tasks that are the highest and best use of my time, allowing me to achieve my goals more efficiently.

Napoleon Hill wrote, "Whatever the mind can conceive and believe, it can achieve." He meant it to show that you can achieve anything you can think of and really believe in. Unfortunately, your beliefs can just as easily draw you away from your goals as they can bring you closer to them. If you believe that you are out of shape or all washed up, you are and will continue to be. It is easy to believe that you will continue to fail if you have failed before. It is much harder to believe that you will succeed when you have failed repeatedly. Self-doubt is a big part of the Frustration Energy Cycle. The more you get stuck in it, the more comfortable it becomes, and the more you will want to stay in it. Go back to your reflection on your successes if you need help remembering that you have been successful.

If you do not have an effective mindset to control your thoughts when trying to conquer the Frustration Energy Cycle, you can fall back on the path of least resistance and remain in the cycle. It can be even harder if you have had easy victories when you were younger and were not as successful later in life. We see this with people who tell the same stories over and over about a job they had or about what a great athlete they were, and if they had only done this or that, they wouldn't be where they are now. They have no plan to move forward. They convinced themselves that they missed their chance. These people have a stagnant mindset that keeps them stuck in the Frustration Energy Cycle, and they don't see a way out, so they wallow in the "good ol' days."

A real-life example involves people of my generation who, like me, were in the mortgage industry before the financial crisis. Many of them were successful, but it was more of a global success than an individual success. All ships rise with the high tide. It is when the tide goes out that you see who actually makes it. As the mortgage industry contracted, changed, and became less lucrative, people were scrambling to keep the level of success they had before the decline. They held on to a path that was no longer there. Many of those people landed in jobs that they did not like. They suffered from long-term unemployment and were frustrated. The path they were following disappeared, and they were lost at sea. They were left unprepared and adrift because they had a stagnant mindset. They just rode the wave, hoping it would last forever. When it crashed, they had no place to go. You may not experience a catastrophic meltdown of your industry, but you will likely face economic disruptions that could affect you.

When a crisis occurs, your mindset can make the difference between success and failure. Your mindset can allow you to make a conscious decision. An effective mindset will allow you to be flexible and adapt to changes. Change is never easy. There is uncertainty with change, and uncertainty can cause anxiety. That anxiety can drive you toward familiar paths with the least resistance, in other words, toward mediocrity. An effective mindset can help you fight that anxiety.

Your mindset is built on belief. If you believe you can succeed, you are more likely to do so. The same applies if you believe you will fail. Believing in yourself and your process gives you an advantage in reaching an Authentic Success.

Passively waiting for a change to undo itself and return you to the path you are used to puts you at risk of being dragged down the wrong path. Change can force you forward, which can help you find your new path, but the new path's appearance may not be an instant thing. If you are entrenched in an industry that no longer sustains jobs, you may need to find something else. You may need to backtrack, hop from path to path for a while, or blaze your own trail. There is a good chance that you will experience some kind of crisis at some point in your life. That crisis may be in your career: you may be pigeonholed at your job, laid off, or fired, or your whole industry may change or disappear. You need to be pragmatic and ready to change when the time comes. You cannot control your job, but you can control your career. It is this type of adaptable mindset that can get you through the crisis. A crisis does not need to be catastrophic to have a negative impact on your life. Minor crises in your day can throw you off your game and disrupt your mindset. This crisis can appear in many forms and at different levels of severity. Examples include:

§   If you are a teacher and a disruptive student is added to your class

§   If you are planning a trip and you get sick

§   If you were planning to hike the Smoky Mountains and there is a forest fire

Some things happen that are outside of your control. You need to adapt if you are going to achieve your goals. Whether to persevere or succumb to the Frustration Energy Cycle depends on your mindset. What is the state of your mindset right now? If you are like most people, you probably have not thought about it too deeply. Take some time to reflect.

§   What is your level of perseverance?

§   Are you adaptable?

§   How well can you focus on a goal?

Another Factor that can lead you to the Frustration Energy Cycle is a lack of focus. What are you trying to achieve, and are you actually working to achieve it? Lying to ourselves about our level of effort is easy. Continuing with the career example, are you working when you are at work? What value are you adding? Are you investing in your career and adding value to your company? Many people start going through the motions and simply doing what they think their job entails, which is usually just meeting the minimum requirements. Many experienced people retire before they leave their jobs. They have a shorter schedule and look forward to the times when they are not working. They leave tasks undone and add less value than a less experienced and cheaper employee. Having this attitude will hold you back, and you will not be able to achieve your goals.

That lack of focus and persistence can be the main obstacle to becoming an Authentic Achiever. You maintain an adequate level of effort, and you reach a point where you are at the top of the pay scale for your job, and you start to feel insecure. You begin to see that your company can hire people to do your job for a fraction of what they pay you, and the new people may even be able to do it better. These new people have a better grasp of new technology, they have more energy, and they bring a fresh perspective to the job. You are tired, bored, becoming less effective, and possibly a little bitter. Having a stagnant mindset can make you less qualified for your position the longer you stay in it.

If you participate in this in-work retirement and become disengaged from your job, you can suffer mediocrity and may eventually be fired or laid off from your job. None of us is entitled to a job. We are trading services for money. If you fail to provide the necessary service or charge twice what someone else does, you may be vulnerable to being replaced. Success does not necessarily mean promotion. You define what success means to you, so you can hold one job over a career and be successful. Many teachers do just that. If you stay up-to-date with technology, news, and industry trends, you can continue to add value and achieve success. You can be a goldmine to your company and a repository of information, keeping you in demand.

It is the in-work retirement mindset that can lead to the cycle of disengagement. If you have an entitlement mindset and do not invest in yourself, you can become less valuable to your company over time and become more expensive to retain. As you become less valuable and more expensive, you will not have access to opportunities, and may be more vulnerable to layoffs. This lack of access will make it very hard for you to achieve your goals and can lead to the Frustration Energy Cycle. When your mindset does not match your ambition, you risk becoming bitter because you are not achieving your goals. This bitterness can lead to you becoming even more disengaged. This disengagement can spiral to the point where you may even be hostile towards people. Disengagement will lead you to become fully entrenched in the frustration energy cycle.

The key to breaking this cycle is to know that you have control over it. The point may come where you are so bitter that the only remedy is for you to find a new employer. If that is the case, you should do it. If you feel strongly negative about your employer, there is a good chance that your employer can see your bitterness and may not have the confidence in you that they once had. If that is the case, the situation is usually not recoverable. It would be easier and healthier to get a fresh start. If you take control, you can leave on your terms rather than being laid off and left scrambling. A fresh start can be a great place to reinvent your mindset.

We have been using careers as an example because it is easy to relate to, but this disengagement does not just happen at work. You can also become disengaged from family and relationships, which can lead to bitterness and further disconnection. You need to invest in other aspects of your life outside of work life.

If you are not *engaged*, you cannot succeed.

No matter how strong your mindset is, we all experience periods of disengagement in all areas of our lives. It can hit at any time in situations like these:

- § **Career:** We have a bad time at work, and we cannot wait for Friday to come.
- § **Family:** The kids do not do their chores, and you have to rush because people are coming over.
- § **Volunteer Work:** You are bringing Thanksgiving baskets to the unfortunate in your community, and you are assigned to bring a basket to a family that seems better off than you; a house that is bigger than yours, two expensive cars, and a huge TV (true story).

Any of these situations can lead to disengagement. The key is to re-engage quickly. Do something that gets your juices flowing again.

Reinvigorating your mindset can be something as simple as relaxing over the weekend and being ready to take on new challenges the next week. You don't need to overcomplicate it. Reflect on what caused you to be disengaged and work to overcome it or at least persevere through it until you can overcome it. Maintaining an effective mindset will help you continue to show up and achieve your goals.

Eighty percent of success is showing up. Showing up means more than just being there. It is being engaged. You have control over your career even if other people have control of your job. The control you have includes the control over your attitude. One of my mentors shared a story with me. He said that there was a guy who was late to work and stuck in traffic. He was cut off by another driver and spilled coffee all over his car. He was furious, and he kept his anger all day. He couldn't focus during the day and told his story of negativity to everyone he met. What did this get him? He had an unproductive day, failed to accomplish his goals, and made himself appear negative to his coworkers. What happened to the other driver? Nothing. The other driver does not even know our hero exists. He went through his day without a care. Our hero lets someone who did not know he even existed rule his day.

Whose fault was it, our hero's or the offender's? It was our hero's fault. If he had just taken a deep breath and reset his mindset, he would not have had an unproductive day, and he could have laughed about the event at the water cooler rather than complaining about it. His coworkers would have laughed with him rather than commiserating with or being annoyed by him. You control your attitude, and having a good attitude will make it easier to succeed in whatever you want to do.

When you are reinvigorating your mindset, keep in mind that the three keys to breaking free of the Frustration Energy Cycle and getting to your goals involve doing more with what you have now:

1. Add more value than you are adding now and have that value targeted towards your goals.

2. Produce more energy to go beyond what you are doing now. If you are always tired, you will struggle to reach your desired goals. Get yourself in the condition you need to be in to achieve your goals.

3. Position yourself for success. Have the attitude, the diet, the fitness, and the environment to accomplish what you want to accomplish.

We are all service providers, no matter what our profession. You need to add value to the process, or you will be less effective at best and expendable at worst. What are you doing to improve the service you provide? If you want to stand out, you need to perform at a higher level. To do this, you will need to know how your organization values you. How you stand out will differ depending on what you are trying to accomplish.

Remember, you are delivering value to others for the ultimate purpose of benefiting yourself. If no one knows you completed a task, then your delivery of the product to your customer was anonymous, providing no return on your investment. Anonymous work delivers value to others, but only personal satisfaction; otherwise, you receive no additional benefit from it. Anonymous acts work for donations and works of goodwill. It does not work in career development. Just working does not set you apart. Mediocre achievers can work hard, too. You cannot have career development in a vacuum. People need to know that you are effectively accomplishing goals before they will help you progress down your path. An effective mindset can help you treat your efforts as a product and the people around you as your customers. You provide the products people need in exchange for some form of compensation.

If you want to benefit from your work, the value you produce must be delivered. You will find that what is needed is not always something that is wanted. You can add the most value by delivering things that people did not even know they needed or wanted. People may have a vague understanding of what they want/need. If you can translate that want/need into a specific reality, you have added a lot of value and have shown that you are someone worthy of notice.

The concept of need vs want can be a little confusing, so here are some examples of needs that your "customer" may not want:

§   Delivering discipline to your children is a product that the kids need but don't necessarily want.

§   The report you need to complete for your boss is something she wants, but completing a more in-depth analysis shows something she didn't even know she needed

§   Presenting classwork in a way that keeps students engaged is something they needed but did not even know they wanted

The steps you need to take to add value will depend on your goals. What are you willing to do beyond that to get to the next level? You may need to stop doing things you're good at if they're not getting you closer to your goals. I happen to be good at translating business needs into system designs. The problem is that I don't like doing it, and I don't want to take that path. I found myself getting pigeonholed into that kind of work, and that was hurting my chances of achieving the goals I wanted to pursue. Because I had an effective mindset, I was able to break out of the pigeonhole.

To break out of that pigeonhole, I began to focus on the fundamental skills when talking with people about my value:

§   I have led interdepartmental, multiple-discipline projects

§   I have strong analytical skills

§   I have strong communication and writing skills

By employing an adaptable mindset and focusing on the transferability of my skills, I was able to get out of the business area I didn't like and grow into the side of the business that I enjoyed.

Hopefully, you see the value of an effective mindset, but you may be wondering how to develop one. Here are some strategies to develop your mindset.

BUILDING A STRONG MINDSET

The concept of mindset can be confusing, and you may not know how to change your mindset. Like many of the concepts in this book, you can find answers through reflection as discussed in this chapter.

Once you have a general understanding of your current mindset, you can take steps to build a more effective one.

§   Develop your Mindset Foundation: The foundation is based on your values. Examine your moral compass and personality, then determine how you want to proceed and what you are willing to do to achieve your goals. There will be things about yourself that you don't want to change. Determining your base values helps you develop a strong Mindset Foundation.

§   Build your Mindset Frame: Now that you have established your foundation on who you are, it is time to build your Mindset Frame. What attitudes and perspectives do you need to change or reinforce? You have control over your attitude and perspectives. By changing or reinforcing them, you can build the Mindset Frame on which you can grow your mindset. A weak frame bends under pressure; a strong one supports expansion.

§   Growing your Mindset Body: Your Mindset Body is based on your habits. Whether positive or negative, your habits drive your mindset. By developing a strong, positive set of habits, you grow an effective Mindset Body that prepares you to achieve an Authentic Success.

Once your mindset is established, it helps to consider it as a machine or even a living thing. Your mindset will need maintenance. Maintaining your mindset is the same process as building it. Reflecting on where you are, reaffirming your foundation, strengthening your frame, and continuing to grow your mindset body.

Developing an effective mindset is not an easy exercise. It doesn't always work the first time. The good news is that the process is simple. Repeat the process just like you would in maintenance until you develop a mindset that suits your needs.

This exercise offers you many benefits. Once you have an effective mindset, it will:

§   Shield you from toxicity in your environment

§   Provide a reserve fuel tank

§   Allow you to magnify your efforts to get more done faster

§   Give you a navigation system to your goals

Reflection

Will your current mindset help or hinder you on your journey to authentic success?

How does your mindset need to change?

What are you willing to do to develop an effective mindset?

Goals

Document what is good and bad about your mindset.

Actions

Develop a strategy to improve your mindset.

CHAPTER 5

Performance Image

*"Today I will do what others won't,
so tomorrow I can do what others can't."*
–Jerry Rice

*"Fitness is about so much more than exercise.
It is a catalyst for positive change
and it affects every aspect of your life."*
–Amanda Russell

Have you ever read a career development book or a leadership book that discussed your diet and exercise routine? My guess is that you probably haven't, and you may be wondering why I'm bringing up diet and exercise, and what they have to do with your personal success.

In my martial arts training, there is a kata called Sanchin, which means "three battles" and refers to the mind, body, and spirit. Many times, we forget the second battle, our bodies. We invest time in feeding our minds through reading, education, and training. In the last chapter, we talked about working on your mindset (spirit), but what about how you treat your body?

You may have heard the quote, "You never get a second chance to make a first impression." How people see you is a major part of a first impression. Before you say a word, people are judging you. Developing your Performance Image will help you improve that first impression.

We are constantly warned not to judge a book by its cover, but we do anyway. I was an oriental rug salesman in college. A man came in wearing shorts and a shirt, looking as though he had just finished cleaning up a pile of leaves. He drove up in an old Land Rover and wanted to look at rugs. The other salesman did not want to talk with him because they thought he would be a waste of time. It turned out that he was very wealthy and ended up buying $20,000 worth of rugs.

He could afford to look frumpy because he could afford not to be taken seriously. He had other options. If you are working to get your shot, you need to be right and tight every time. When you are pursuing big goals, you cannot afford to miss opportunities by looking lazy, sloppy, or not too bright. Your Performance Image matters. It helps to present yourself in a way that would be accepted by the people you are trying to get something from. When you are getting people to help you achieve your goals, you are selling yourself. You are building your Performance Image. If you're unsure what that looks like, consider examples of how the person is portrayed on TV or in the movies. What does a great teacher look like, what does a great parent look like, or a businessman or scientist? Focus on the image, not the looks. You do not need to look like Brad Pitt or Jennifer Aniston to be successful, but how do they dress, and how do they hold themselves? That is how people expect a successful person to look. How you look and act builds your Performance Image.

We all judge with our eyes. Who looks like they have more energy, an Olympic sprinter or the guy at the picnic with a big gut and no shirt? That does not make the guy at the picnic less competent in his profession, but it does give the Olympic sprinter an advantage with first impressions. Can we succeed if we don't look fit? Yes, we can. Does being unfit constitute a self-inflicted obstacle? Yes, it does. As I have said several times before, we need every advantage we can get.

Fitness is generally in our control. If we can, we should overcome that self-inflicted obstacle. I have been significantly overweight at various times and relatively fit at other times. I have transitioned back and forth so many times that my Performance Image reflects that I have always just lost some weight.

You have a Performance Image right now, whether you know it or not. Are you the person people always call when an important task needs to be done? Or do people roll their eyes when you are assigned to their project team? People see you in a certain way, just as they see the brand of paper towels they buy at the store. Are you worth the extra money? Do you clean up the mess or push the mess around and fall apart? How the people around you perceive you is your Performance Image. Are you someone people are attracted to or repelled by? You can influence how people react to you.

If you do not control that Performance Image, you will be at the mercy of what other people think. I know a person who has a lot of experience and can add value with their knowledge, but is afraid to state a firm opinion, which leads him to talk in circles. His tendency to talk in circles leads his manager and peers to discount his opinion and not take him seriously. This flaw has put a ceiling above him, and as he grows older and loses energy, he will struggle to succeed in his current position. He may even face difficulties maintaining his current job level. That person does not control his Performance Image, and his brand screams annoying and mediocre. What does your brand portray?

In building your Performance Image, it helps to manage your weight the best you can. I know that it's not easy, but it doesn't mean you have to be athletic. Consider getting fit enough to have confidence, dress appropriately, and act the part you want to play. You sometimes have to "fake it before you make it," so don't be discouraged. If you are overweight or cannot afford appropriate clothes, you can still succeed; it's just harder. Try to take all the advantages you can. If you are allowed to wear shorts and T-shirts in the office, it does not mean that you should. Consider this example. If you are going to a doctor who has more credibility, the doctor in shorts and a T-shirt or the doctor in a lab coat? How can you build and maintain your credibility?

There are already enough obstacles. You cannot afford to add your own. It's best to present yourself in a way that portrays the brand you want people to see. If you are overweight and get winded walking up the stairs, people will notice, and that will not help you establish yourself as the up-and-coming manager, the active parent, or the most helpful volunteer.

Overweight people also have fewer fashion choices. Often, the selection is less flattering than the options available to fit people, which can further prejudice your Performance Image. If you appear overweight and frumpy, you will look even less like the leader you aspire to be. This is not just the case for business success. It is everywhere. If you are trying to obtain educational services for your child and you show up at school wearing stretched-out sweatpants and an oversized polo shirt, people will not take you as seriously as they would if you were wearing a dress shirt and slacks. It's the same whether you're buying a car or any other large purchase. The person you are buying from will look at you, and that first impression will determine the level of service you receive. It's not fair, but it's reality, and it will hold you back.

When I was young, I was an insurance agent. I was sent to an insurance company for training, and during that time, I had a session that I vividly remember to this day, over thirty years later. One of the insurance trainers introduced a successful insurance executive. When introducing the executive, the leader said, "This man is a gentleman; he is always wearing a suit." That struck me. Wearing a suit does not make a man a gentleman, but it gives the appearance of being a gentleman. A person dressed professionally is what people see as a gentleman; how we present ourselves matters.

Hitting the gym can help you in your career. You may want to consider developing a fitness routine. Fitness helps in a couple of ways. If you look fit, you will be treated with more respect. It's not fair, but that's the way it is. People judge with their eyes. If you are overweight or even hold yourself in a way that makes you look flabby, people may look upon you as slow and lower energy than someone who is fit. Your appearance can put you at an immediate disadvantage. From my experience, being cognizant of what you eat is also very important. Junk food can slow you down and drain your energy. It may also put you in the bathroom rather than an important impromptu meeting. Eating healthy will help you get the energy you need to meet your challenges. When we have bad diets and are in high-stress situations, we can find ourselves getting sick. Whether it is recurrent sinus infections or irritable bowel syndrome, we can find ourselves out of commission. When I was younger, I suffered from some of these ailments. It is hard to succeed if you are in the bathroom during important meetings or if you are out sick when important decisions are being made. Eighty percent of success is showing up; if you aren't there, you will miss out on opportunities.

A major example of this situation in my life occurred about twenty years ago. I was very sick on the day of an important meeting where I had an important role to play. I decided to call in sick. My absence left the company president in a difficult position. My calling in sick had a very negative impact on my future with that company. Before the meeting I missed, I was given important assignments on key projects. After I called in sick that day, I found that my assignments were not as important and were instead focused on ancillary projects. I was sidelined, and my career stalled. If I could do it over again, I would have medicated myself, gone in that day, and taken the next day off.

Since we cannot go back in time, I persevered. I left that company and got a fresh start. I learned from that experience and now know that when I have responsibility for a task, I need to see that it gets done. I don't necessarily need to do it myself, but I make sure it gets done. That mistake set me back a couple of years in my career. I needed to build it back up. I was still a hard worker, and I still brought in results, but that one sick day defined how people who were important in the company saw me for years to come. It is not just about hard work; it is about the proper image, and many of us don't have the experience when we are younger, and we stumble along. Some are lucky or have received training, allowing them to avoid the pitfalls. The rest of us have setbacks that keep us from getting to where we want to go. By continuing to perform well and persevering, I was able to find success and overcome the obstacles. It would have been easier to be bitter and blame others, but by keeping positive and taking action, I was able to succeed.

To avoid the Frustration Energy Cycle and succeed at whatever you have chosen to do, it helps to have the energy to get the job done. Plans without action do not achieve goals, and actions take energy. If you want something different from what you have now, you need to do something different. Unfortunately, you probably can't just drop what you are doing for a living to achieve your other goals, so you need to do more to get what you want. That means, if you are in that situation, you will need to accomplish both your work and other goals to achieve your Authentic Success, and to do that, you need energy for long days and increased effort.

"To be successful, you must accept all challenges that come your way. You can't just accept the ones you like."
–Mike Gafka

As we previously discussed, energy is a crucial factor in achieving success. It is not only the ability to get more done, but it is also the Performance Image showing you have energy. If people think you have energy, they are more likely to offer you more responsibilities and opportunities. Although I'm currently on the less fit side of my ups and downs, I've managed to maintain an energetic appearance through my involvement in martial arts and a regular training routine. This appearance does have an expiration date. Suppose I cannot maintain my level of energy or remain unfit for too long. In that case, I can fall into a negative health cycle and lose my Performance Image of having energy, which might compromise my advantage.

When people carry extra weight, especially as they age, they tend to tire more easily. This can lead to a negative health cycle, where they lose fitness and change their habits to compensate for their lack of physical activity. They start waiting for parking spaces near the store, taking the elevator or escalator, even for just one floor. They also avoid working out. Furthermore, they often have other responsibilities that become obstacles to working out, so they avoid it.

We can also fool ourselves about what eating healthy means. We eat too much, and we make high-calorie choices. These foods can stay with us, and their digestion takes even more energy. Have you been exhausted after eating a large, unhealthy meal? It is hard to get work done after that. If you add alcohol to the mix, it is even harder.

It's hard to get things done when you're sick and tired. Have you ever gone out for a few beers on a Friday night and had to do a cumbersome chore like mowing the lawn on Saturday morning? Especially if you were out later and drank more than you normally do, you are probably not very motivated to work on Saturday morning. You feel tired, a little heavy, and your brain is foggy. Now let's change that work from mowing the lawn to doing your taxes or preparing an important client presentation. How capable are you?

We tend to do this to ourselves every day. It may not be as extreme as drinking all night, but we do sabotage ourselves. We overeat takeout food and stay up late watching Netflix before a client meeting. We don't exercise and end up wearing uncomfortable, tight clothing all day. We sabotage our success by adding obstacles and distractions to our everyday lives. These obstacles are so commonplace that we often think of them as part of our lives, rather than as things that we can fix.

It is almost cliché to talk about how our energy can diminish as we go through the day. There are commercials for products aimed at addressing people who get tired around 3:00 p.m. every day. People rationalize the energy drain and say it's because we're getting old, rather than looking at it and seeing that it's because they had a heavy lunch. Society will tell you to douse yourself with caffeine all morning, when the cause was staying up late watching TV and eating pizza. These eating habits sabotage your success. It's hard to be productive when your mind is foggy from a bad diet or if you're feeling sick and tired.

If we analyze it, most of us will find that at least some of our fatigue and sickness are self-inflicted. We do not get enough sleep, we eat too much, we eat the wrong things, and we avoid exercise. These habits can destroy our energy, especially as we get older. I was out with some friends. It is okay to go out with friends and drink and eat poorly as long as you know the opportunity cost. My night out cost me a productive morning. Diet choices have consequences. If you make intentional decisions, you can have fun and avoid missing opportunities.

There is no off-season. If you played sports as a kid, you may have been able to take it easy in the off-season. You would work really hard for the season, and when it was over, you would take a break. As we get older, we can't afford an off-season. We need to be consistent in our quest for health. With all the things going on in your life and your body's resistance to change, taking an offseason puts you behind, and it can be very hard to catch up. I picture life as canoeing upstream. If you stop paddling, you get swept back downstream. As you get older, the stream gets faster. You need to keep paddling if you want to continue doing what you want to do. If you stop, you may find yourself just getting further and further from your goal. If you are not growing, you are dying.

You can set yourself apart from your competition by being in a little better shape and having a bit more energy. Think of life as a horse race. The winner gets a prize twice as large as the runner-up, and the runner-up gets a larger prize than the third-place winner. Did the winner work twice as hard as the runner-up and four times as hard as the third place? No. Many times, there is a race to the finish. The first, second, and third-place winners are right on top of each other. Inches make the difference. The winner can be 1 inch ahead of the other two horses to win. It can be the smallest of margins that can keep us from having the success we desire. Giving yourself every advantage you can is important because your success may require you to get ahead one more inch than your peers can go.

You have work, personal obligations, and other commitments. If you choose to have a fitness routine, you only have a certain amount of time to work out, so it helps to be consistent, so you don't lose what you've built. Have you ever worked on a computer document for hours only to realize you forgot to save it when your computer crashed? How did that feel? If you're like me, you're angry at the computer and yourself. Also, if you did not allow yourself enough time to complete the task, you are now behind the eight ball and are under a lot of stress. The same goes for your body.

If you postponed getting in shape, ate a heavy meal, and had a few drinks the night before a big meeting, and you get to the convention hall only to realize you must walk nearly a half mile to get to your appointment, what happens? From my experience, I'll tell you that you arrive at your meeting out of breath and sweaty. If you are meeting someone for the first time, how does that look? At the time, I was lucky. I got there early, so I was able to wash up a bit and catch my breath before the meeting, but I felt sweaty in my suit all day. It was a distraction I could not afford.

It is not just for business. If you are out of shape and there is an emergency like evacuating a stadium or an airport, are you ready to make the walk to safety? Would you be able to walk down ten flights of stairs, then run a half mile to safety? If not, how will you handle an emergency? What if you are a parent or guardian with little kids in an amusement park? Would you be able to walk the entire length of the park and make it to your car? That is a requirement for a thunderstorm. Again, from my experience, I can tell you that a lack of fitness makes this experience more stressful than it needs to be.

Your fitness is not just important for your success. It is also vital for your longevity. My friends and I were joking that we would be able to retire about three years after we die. Many of us will not be able to or will not want to retire at the traditional age. Are you in good enough shape now to believe that you could continue working when you are seventy? If not, what are you going to do if you reach sixty-five and you realize that you don't have enough money to retire? Even if you are a prudent saver, things can happen that would require you to continue working. You may also want to continue working.

As an Authentic Achiever, you may not hit your stride until you are in your late fifties. You may find yourself at sixty-eight loving what you do and not even imagining retirement. Will you have the stamina to continue? Of course, there are unexpected health issues that could curtail our ability to continue, but in general, are you setting yourself up for continued success, or for disappointment and failure later in life? Consider the present and the future. There are both short-term and long-term benefits of fitness. Also, you are never too old to start. If you are in your fifties or sixties, it is not too late to get healthy. It may be harder than it would have been in your thirties, but it is still worth the time and effort. You get the same short and long-term benefits.

My father passed away shortly before I wrote this book. He was overweight and sedentary, which led to the contraction of multiple comorbidities. Because of his health problems, he needed to have major high-risk surgery, which ultimately led to his passing away. He chose to ignore his doctor's advice on maintaining his health, which carried a heavy cost.

As we have been discussing, we tend to judge people and use fitness level as one of those factors. These judgements can be driven by comparisons. During my father's health crisis, I started making comparisons between my father and one of my mentors. My mentor is of a similar age to my father but has a fitness routine. He also needed surgery, but because of his fitness and mobility, he was not high risk and was able to make a smooth recovery.

Comparisons are unfair. There were factors that may not have been fixed by a fitness routine, but this example taught me that having one can help preserve my ability to achieve goals in the future.

Expectations are the first step towards or away from an opportunity. If you and other people expect you to succeed, you have more of a chance of succeeding. Underdogs succeed, too, but they believe in themselves and set high expectations for themselves. These expectations are helped or hindered by your level of fitness.

It's hard to expect yourself to succeed if you struggle to get out of bed, get winded walking up the stairs, or have to unbutton your pants to tie your shoes. You will think of yourself differently from the person who gets up early and goes for a run. To be fair, it may not be easy to be the person who gets up early for a run. They may not have the same scheduling issues you do. Using myself as an example, I knew many people who exercised daily, but they had different circumstances than I did. When I started my fitness routine, I had to commute forty miles each way in traffic to my job. Could I have gotten a job closer? Not if I wanted to keep the lifestyle I wanted for my family and stay in the industry I have worked in for over twenty years.

To remain fit, I needed much more discipline than the guys with less grueling schedules. I knew who would go running in the morning. I would wave to them as I was driving to work because I needed to leave so much earlier than they did. That is when I started to get up at 4:45 a.m. every morning. I would do some warm-up exercises and prepare for the day. After taking a productivity class, I incorporated inspirational reading and writing into my morning routine. This was not a perfect solution. I am still in better physical condition than many of my peers, but I am not where I want to be. Having been in better shape, I know that I could have more energy and accomplish more if I were to return to my ideal physical condition.

Yes, I want to get fit for myself. I want to be healthy, and I want to be able to do more things when I get older, but I also want to send a message. I want the people around me to know that I have the energy, persistence, and determination to help them and, through that work, succeed myself. Besides the actual work you do, how you behave outside the job sends a message to the people around you. When you have big goals, you want to signal to the people around you that you are more than the job you are in now. If you are not, then why would anyone consider you for something bigger? Again, this is not just about a career. If you are known as an active, informed parent, the teacher will be more responsive in your parent-teacher meetings. If you are able to move around with ease, you can be a more active volunteer. If you can stay on your feet all day, you can be more involved as a teacher.

The expectations people have of you also make a difference.

§   If you come into your office late every day because you have trouble waking up and getting to the job, that sends a message

§   If you are walking with your boss, talking, and you get out of breath, that sends a message

§   If you get home from work and don't have the energy to interact with family and friends, that sends a message

The longer that you send that message, the more that expectation is set, and it becomes part of your Performance Image. There have been times in my life when the expectation my kids had was that Dad is always tired. I would spend time with my kids, but I wouldn't be fully present. Work or financial stress would always be in the background, and even though they were little, they had expectations of what I was capable of doing.

Everyone will have expectations of you, positive or negative, just like you have expectations of others. To build new expectations, you need to improve your Performance Image, which takes energy. Unless you can afford to make drastic life changes, you will need to find more time and energy to go above and beyond what you are doing now. To build more energy, you need to be fit. Eating properly and getting moderate exercise will provide you with the energy to be a better worker, be able to be more present when you get home, to take that self-paced MS Excel class at night, and to get up early enough to prepare for your day and get to work on time. You do not need to be a marathon runner or a CrossFit champion to have more energy. Eating healthier and working out a few times a week will get you where you need to be.

Since this book already suggested that you add a lot more to your schedule, it may seem strange that I am asking you to work out too. Working out may seem like another obstacle rather than a means to succeed. To be successful, we need to get more done; we all have a limited amount of time. You may ask, can't we just skip the workout? I suggest that you think of your workout as maintenance for both your mind and body. If you never took the time to change the oil in your car and bought the wrong kind of gas for your car, how long would your car last? You would have car problems, expensive problems, very soon. Unlike your car, you can't buy a new body every five years.

If you are going to push your mind and body, you need to maintain your body. To maintain it, you need to exercise and eat properly. Just like your car, your body will only perform for a short period when you push yourself with a bad diet and lack of fitness, but not for long. Did you ever have your week "catch up to you"? You work really hard all week, sneak junk food at breaks, and then need the weekend to recover? You ran yourself into the ground. You can only do that for so long before you start breaking down.

Military personnel train all the time. They exercise outside of their normal duties. My son is in the National Guard. Even when he is off duty, he runs with a weighted backpack to stay prepared. That keeps him sharp and ready to react and go the extra mile. We need to do the same. We need to train our bodies to work and endure. Exercise is getting more important with the ability to retire at sixty-five becoming less realistic. If you need to be working at seventy to maintain your lifestyle, you better have the energy and health to do it.

Consider treating fitness as an investment. Your time is valuable. You need to make the most of your time. We are all given twenty-four hours a day. How you invest that time determines how successful you can be. The workout can seem frivolous and unimportant, and a good thing to cut out. However, if you view fitness as an investment, you will better understand how important fitness is. You can compare it to your money. You need money to spend now, money for a rainy day, and money for retirement. The same can be said about fitness.

§   You need the energy fitness gives you today

§   You need the quicker recovery time fitness brings when you are sick

§   You need the future energy to do what you want to do when you are retired

This investment is one of time and a series of deliberate actions. To be consistent, it helps to allocate some time each day to exercise.

It also helps to deliberately think about your diet. It is easy to fall into the habit of grabbing junk food to satisfy cravings rather than eating for nutrition. You can still eat tasty food, but it is better if it is healthy and in moderation.

Each time you eat healthily and exercise, you are making an investment in your future. You are working hard now, and when you succeed, you will want to keep what you've gotten. If you work hard and meet your goal, you don't want to lose it because you have run out of energy or you have gotten sick. Investing in your health now will help you mitigate the risks of future health issues. It's best if the fitness plan is determined by your current health and fitness levels. Don't try to go beyond your level right away. It took time to get into the condition you are in, and it will take time to get into the condition you want to be in.

At this point, you may face one of your biggest obstacles: feeling shame. You may feel insecure or even embarrassed by your physical condition. Having your stomach hang over your pants or getting winded by a simple walk can make you feel bad about yourself and make it easier to ignore the health concern than to face the problem. Your initial workouts may be harder than you expected, and you may feel uncomfortable doing them. It may even feel like you are not ready to start. To overcome this obstacle, you will need to be satisfied with doing the activity poorly until you are able to do it well.

There is no reason to feel ashamed. You've experienced life situations that have led you to where you are now, and you're now seeking something different. Be proud that you are willing to face the uncertainty of doing something new and pursuing your big goals.

To boost and maintain energy, you need the proper fuel. If you feed your body junk food, you will not have the energy to keep going. Unhealthy food puts a drag on energy. You may get an early boost from it, but you feel tired and heavy later. That heavy feeling can prevent you from going for a walk or working out. It can also cloud your mind, making your mind sluggish and slower to respond to stimuli. By having a poor diet, you are sabotaging your energy and, in turn, sabotaging your ability to succeed. If you know any people with diabetes, you can see how an imbalance of sugar can change them. This happens to a lesser degree in people with healthier sugar levels. Diet has a direct effect on how one feels and how one reacts to situations. Bad diet choices can have a negative effect on your attitude and on how well you work and sleep, which can also sabotage your attitude.

Working out releases endorphins, which can make you feel better and give you needed energy. Being more mobile also helps you feel better. I am in inadequate shape but am looking to improve. When I am with my peers, I can do a lot of things they cannot, and they blame their age, even though they are younger than me. If I can do things that people younger than me can't, it is not age that is keeping them from doing it. It is the level of fitness that keeps them from doing it. Now I am a lot less fit than I was three years ago. Is it because I've hit some age threshold and it's all downhill from here? No, it is because I have not made fitness a priority for myself over the last three years. It is funny because one of my peers who complained about age has now surpassed me in fitness because he made fitness a priority. Now he is helping me get motivated to get back on the fitness track.

It also helps to include flexibility. It is not just a function of the mind. It is also a function of the body.

I was at a conference after a bad flight and a bad night's sleep. At that time, I had gained a bit of weight, and my flexibility was not what it should have been. I dropped my notebook in the hotel lobby, and it took a bit of effort to pick it up. The bellman actually came running over to help me. Thankfully, I picked it up before he got there, so I wasn't too embarrassed by my difficulties picking up my notebook.

It is not strength or speed that makes you feel younger; it is flexibility. Being able to bend over and tie your shoes without having to sit down or pick up the notebook without an issue are all things that make you feel better about yourself and give you the confidence to do things that you may have considered yourself too old to do in the past. It's about believing you can do something that actually helps you accomplish it. If you need to meet twenty people over three days at a conference, your ability to walk the miles back and forth in the convention center and be able to sit down and stand up with ease sets you apart from your peers. We need to be flexible enough to play the hand dealt to us. There will be people who have an easier time than we do. It is not fair, but it is reality. We need to be flexible enough to roll with the punches and be determined enough to reach our goals.

Overindulgence in fitness can be dangerous, too. Check with your doctor before you start exercising. Build your fitness over time. It took you years to get out of shape. You are not going to get fit overnight.

We can't always control our physical condition. If someone is in a wheelchair or has another disability, they can still succeed; it is just harder. It is one more obstacle that needs to be overcome.

Reflection

What is the condition of your Performance Image?
What can you do to improve your Performance Image?
What are you willing to do?

Goals

Document your perceptions of your Performance Image.

Actions

Develop a strategy to improve your Performance Image.

CHAPTER 6

The Intentionally Sharpened Mind

"Opportunities don't happen. You create them."
—Chris Grosser

"Whenever you see a successful person, you only see the public glories; never the private sacrifices that led to their success."
—Vaibhav Shah

Learning is an investment of the limited resource of time. If you are going to develop your Intentionally Sharpened Mind, you will need to intentionally allocate the time to learn. Like working out, learning can appear to be optional. Something that can be put off until someday.

As we've discussed earlier in the book, to achieve your Authentic Success, you need to be on top of your game, and one key factor to being on top of your game is intentional learning.

You don't need to jump into learning with both feet. You can ease into it and build realistic habits that fit your schedule. As you recognize the value and understand that the investment of time does not have a negative impact on the rest of your life, you can add more to your learning habits.

There is an amazing variety of opportunities to learn. The internet and content creators have built powerful tools for learners. No matter what your learning style, you can find something that fits into your schedule.

We talked about the two-edged sword of experience. Keeping this sword sharp and effective on your success journey takes an Intentionally Sharp Mind. If you don't keep learning, you can stagnate and become less adaptable to new situations. Learning can include things like:

§   Reading books and articles—reading is the original self-paced course

§   Traditional education—taking classes and attending seminars

§   Informational interviews—finding someone who has the knowledge you want and asking them for advice, guidance, and other sources of information

§   Mentor/protégé and coaching relationships—building a relationship with people who have expertise in the field you want to pursue can give you access to the knowledge you need to succeed

The people around you can offer an education that is not available in any classroom. They can share their life experiences, which provide you with intentionally acquired experiences that help you achieve your goals. The more you know or have experience with, the better equipped you will be to achieve an Authentic Success. It can take a long time to gain experience, but there is a shortcut to acquiring the knowledge that experience brings more quickly. It is to learn from the experience of others. We will go over how you can leverage this source of knowledge.

You can not only learn from others' successes to improve your performance, but you can also learn what to avoid from their mistakes. Learning from other people's mistakes is a shortcut to success. If you can avoid pitfalls, you will move forward more quickly. You can learn about other people's mistakes in several ways:

1. **You can see it firsthand.** You can see what your boss, coworkers, or other peers do and the results they achieve. It may seem like common sense, but if your coworkers are doing something that doesn't work, you should do something else. It can be easy to get caught up and go with the flow or be afraid to rock the boat, but if you want to succeed, you need to do the things that work.

2. **You can learn from mentors and coaches.** They have their own experience and the experiences of the other people they have mentored. One of the benefits of having a mentor is that you can ask questions. You can't ask a book questions, and in classes, you can't always spend a long time on a specific topic; the teacher needs to move on. Mentors provide you with the specifics you need to make informed decisions.

3. **You can supplement what you learned by reading about people's experiences in books.** Both fiction and non-fiction expose you to situations that can happen to you. Non-fiction, such as biographies and books on your profession or avocation, will often include examples of people making mistakes. These are real-life situations from which you can learn. We can also learn lessons from fiction. These lessons are more general since they do not involve real-life examples, but they are useful.

All of these learning methods help you build an Intentionally Sharpened mind by providing techniques to get ahead more effectively, and a process that can help you establish learning habits, which can give you a sense of accomplishment and keep you motivated. Your education is your responsibility. If you make education a priority, you will find it easier to remain open-minded and accept the opportunity costs of studying. You will stay flexible and be better able to succeed, giving you an advantage over your competitors. You will leverage the experience you have while retaining the curiosity and learning potential of a new employee—a powerful combination. If you know there is always something to learn, you can remain as excited as a student on their first day of class.

If you decide that you will proceed with a strategy for an Intentionally Sharpened Mind, then you do need to make a commitment. You still have a life, so you have to account for your other routines and responsibilities. You need to work, spend time with your friends and family, and take care of your home. There are things you don't need to do. You don't need to watch TV, surf the web, or play games on your phone. You need to decide what you are willing to sacrifice to make the time you need to learn. If you take the time to improve your life, you will reap the rewards, but if you fill your life with empty activities, you will end up with unsatisfying results.

The easiest way to start your learning journey is by reading. You can start off reading for twenty minutes a day. The book can go anywhere you want to go, and if you have an e-book, you can even read it on your phone. Although it is not exactly reading, you can listen to audiobooks while driving or engaging in other activities.

You don't need to spend any money to start. Libraries are still a thing and provide books in all formats, including audiobooks. You don't need to be intimidated if you haven't read books in a while; most books are written to be easily understood. Once you establish yourself as a reader and start reading more technical books, it is easy to look up words you don't understand on your phone. I always have my phone at hand to look up words or concepts I don't understand while I am reading. This is not school; there is no cheating. There is no reason to hold yourself back by not using all the tools you have.

Reading technical books can equip you with the work skills you need to succeed. These can be anything from public speaking books to computer programming guides. For example, if your job requires you to have Excel skills, it makes sense to get a book on using Excel to quickly get the skills you need to get your job done. There are also soft skills, such as interacting with others and leadership. These books can cover everything from selling to spreadsheets to personal development to raising chickens. Whatever skill you need, there is a book out there on it.

Since you are reading this book, you already see the value in reading books for learning new things. Consider making the reading of this book the beginning of a reading habit. Building a habit of consistent reading will help you learn at a fast pace. One of my coaches once told me that you need to read about 30 books to get a Ph.D. in a subject, so if you read thirty books on a subject, you have done the equivalent of a Ph.D. study. That may be a bit of an exaggeration, but there is a material point to it. Reading 30 books on a subject gives you a substantial amount of information on the subject. Since the average person does not read that much (the median number is 4 to 5 books a year at the time of this writing, and almost a quarter of all adults read no books), by reading 30 books, you make yourself an expert in the subject as compared to your peers.

Think about what you can learn if you started reading today to expand your knowledge base. If you're rediscovering reading as a learning source, aim to read one book a month. At the end of the year, you will have read twelve books. If you read a lot now, aim to double your reading pace. I happen to read a lot, and I also listen to audiobooks. By surrounding myself with books, I always keep reading at the front of my mind. I try to read in all formats I can. I have an e-reader, but I also buy books, both hardcover and softcover, as well as audio. Periodicals can also get you information in bite-sized pieces, but they do not dig deep enough into the story to get you a solid understanding of a subject. I started tracking my reading on GoodReads.com. It helps me set goals, and Goodreads provides recommendations for similar books, allowing me to discover books I might have missed in a traditional search.

Reading keeps your mind fresh. You don't need to read stuffy technical tomes that even a proficient reader can only read three pages before getting tired. There are many styles of books, and some subjects and styles that might surprise you. The act of reading helps build your skills. Reading for education doubles that experience by allowing you to practice a skill while learning new information. By doubling down, you are really leveraging your time. In time, you may find that you enjoy reading so you can use it as a source of recreation, tripling your effectiveness by training your brain to absorb information, learn new things, and relax.

The subject you are reading does not have to be an exact match of your study topic. A book on politics can help you in your business career. A book on arts and crafts can help you with teaching. A book on manufacturing can teach you about process control. A book on military actions can teach you about strategy. You will also find that expanding your reading base will open up areas of curiosity that will help you identify what you may want to be doing for your career. Learning is fundamental, and reading can be the first step toward a broader base of learning.

There is a surprising place to learn examples of different situations, a variety of personality types, and how to handle them: reading fiction. Fiction gives you the opportunity to see people in different situations and observe how they act. Regardless of whether the story takes place on the battlefield, in space, at a romantic restaurant, or in a workplace, the characters will find themselves in various situations. You even have books like Animal Farm or Watership Down that use animals as avatars for people. These books can teach you about expectations for situations you have never experienced and how people interact with each other successfully.

I enjoy reading fiction. It helps me relax, and it keeps my mind stimulated. Even though I don't expect to be fighting in an intergalactic battle, I have gained different perspectives on how to lead people and how they react to stressful situations. These are skills that I need for everyday interactions. For the character, the stress may be the warship engine blowing up. In real life, it can be a person who is having trouble with a career-changing presentation. If you have never comforted someone who had a loved one die, having read about it in a fictional account can give you a baseline to start with. You can find examples on how to talk to your child about a failure to make a sports team or to a student on how to bounce back from a failed test performance from characters in books you've read.

Fiction gives you access to life experiences that you have not and sometimes cannot have. The more life experiences you have, the better you will be at dealing with situations as they come up. These fictional life experiences can also help with the flexibility we talked about in an earlier chapter. You will be able to see situations from different perspectives. In a pirate book, you can see from the perspective of the deckhand, the pirate, or the pursuing naval captain, all in one place. If you are a leader, it is important for you to be able to see the world through the eyes of your followers. If you are a worker or an aspiring leader, it is very important for you to see things from the eyes of your leaders. You need to be able to serve your constituency. You can serve more effectively if you can see the world as your constituents do. Fiction offers you the opportunity to have new perspectives without the experience you would need to learn it on your own.

The truth can be stranger than fiction. Another great place to learn from the experiences of others is through biographies. We can only experience so much in our own lives. We live in a particular time and a particular part of the world. We cannot go back in time, and we may not be able to uproot to live in another part of the world. These experiences are not available to us personally, but they are available to us through the eyes of others.

Reading biographies can allow us to experience the lives of other people and learn from their successes and failures. If you want to learn about perseverance, read about Abraham Lincoln or Thomas Edison. If you want to read about tenacity and adventure, Marco Polo may be your man. Books about events can also be helpful. If you want to learn about project management, read about the construction of the Panama Canal. If you want to see how leaders interact, read *1920, The Year of the Six Presidents*.

The person you are reading about does not need to be an exact match of the characteristics you'd like to emulate. I really like Teddy Roosevelt. I have read many books about him, and I emulate some of the traits he exhibited. I was attracted to and learned from his leadership style and how he interacted with the politicians and businesspeople around him. He was not a perfect example of what I wanted to emulate. He did some things that I find despicable. I don't emulate those traits. One of the benefits of the biography is that you know that the deeds were actually done. It teaches you that the goal is achievable, which can help you achieve your goals because you see that it is possible to succeed. Reading about people and events will supplement your experiences without requiring you to live through them. Now, these learned experiences are not necessarily as powerful as lived experiences. We all remember as kids and teenagers that our parents or teachers would tell us that it was a bad idea to do something. They shared their experience with us, but we didn't listen, and as a result, we often received the poor results they had warned us about. We needed to experience it for ourselves. Just reading about it or being told about it won't always satisfy your need for understanding. Sometimes you need to stick your own toes in the water or dive right in. It is not enough to be told that the water is cold. Sometimes you need to feel the water yourself.

In cases where we need to experience something, the biography may inspire us to action. We may never have considered taking a leave of absence to drive across the country or to walk the Appalachian Trail, but a book might inspire us to do so. We may not even know that certain experiences exist. We may not know about zip lines through the jungles of Costa Rica or hiking trails in Southeast Asia. Reading can open our minds to other opportunities.

There are times, however, when the biography will open our minds through the experiences of others. You can learn from and use the experiences of another, and you can actually have an epiphany. You have a lot of experience. If you rely solely on your experience, you only have your perspective to leverage. You may not see how your experiences connect or how you can use them to get ahead. When you see experiences from the lives of other people, you gain a different perspective and can discover potential in yourself that you never thought you had.

You will probably read about people that you like but consider reading about people you don't like. Politics is a great example. People can feel very strongly about politics. If you are reading about American presidents and only read about Theodore Roosevelt, Ronald Reagan, and other Republicans, while leaving out Truman and John F. Kennedy, you are only getting a partial picture. You are not looking at the world from another perspective. If you are partisan, it is even more important for you to read about people from the opposing party. If you don't, you can get blinded by your own feelings.

The same goes for other subjects. If you are going to read about Edison, it helps to also read about Tesla. If you are going to read about combustion engines, you may also want to read about steam engines. Read not only about your religion, but also about other religions. Expand your horizons. The more perspectives you can see from, the better you can relate to more people. You will have a better understanding of how to work with those people. You will be able to serve them better, and in return, you will be better able to succeed. One of my favorite motivational speakers said the best way to get what you want is to get enough other people what they want. You will only be able to give them what they want if you know what they want. You can better know what they want by understanding them as people. To understand them, you need to be able to see the world through their eyes.

There are also the bestselling books out there, and they are bestselling for a good reason. They offer the most people the information they need, but there is also another group of books. With the advent of online shopping, many more books have become available to everyone. This comprehensive marketplace has allowed lesser-known authors to publish their work. The quality of writing can vary, but these books are often very helpful because they are written by the people who do the work, rather than professional writers. These books are cheap and plentiful. They are so cost-effective that you can get only one idea from reading the book and feel good about your investment.

I have a subscription that allows me to "borrow" this class of e-books for a flat monthly fee. The subscription gives me the opportunity to audition books. I can look through it to see if the book has what I am looking for, then read it in depth. If I'm not satisfied with the writing quality or it doesn't meet my expectations, I simply return it and choose another book. This service gives me the freedom to explore books and see what information is out there. This service is very helpful for more obscure subjects.

Reading also helps in nonwork activities. I train in martial arts, so self-defense is one of the skills I enjoy studying. There are a lot of books out there on self-defense. Some teach theory, some teach techniques. Having access to those books has given me a source of information that we didn't have twenty years ago. It is easy and often inexpensive to access the information you need to grow. You just need to look for it.

All these reading strategies take one thing to work. You need to read the books. It can be on an e-reader or a traditional book. Use whatever you feel comfortable with. You are reading this book, which shows you are open to the concept. Spending more time reading will offer you great benefits. It may be time to turn off the TV and read. It is very hard to do that these days with all of the distractions you can encounter.

As I am writing this, it is 5:30 a.m. in the morning, and my phone is already buzzing. I need to make a decision. Do I keep writing, or do I feed my electronics addiction and check my phone? Since I have committed to writing this book, I left my phone until after I was done. You should consider doing the same if you want to achieve the results.

There used to be periodicals that would do deep dives into a subject. They dealt with history, science, business, and other topics. These have generally been replaced by online newsletters and podcasts. Podcasts can be looked at as audio magazines. So even though they are not technically reading, it is close enough for this book. I would be remiss if I didn't at least mention these sources of learning. The political and social podcasts get the most notoriety, but there are subject-specific podcasts that can supplement your education.

If you prefer reading, there are newsletter providers and social media sources that offer articles on the topics you're interested in. If you're interested in video content, you can explore live presentations and other videos on video-sharing sites and social media platforms. Alternatively, if you prefer audio, there are thousands of podcasts to choose from. The flow of information is greater than at any other time in history. You have it at your fingertips. Take advantage of these sources to help you achieve your goals.

When we talk about learning, you probably think of school. More than likely, most of your learning happened in some kind of classroom. A traditional class is a great way to learn. From youth, we are programmed that a classroom is a place to learn, but we are not all made of time and money. When we are struggling to put food on the table, it can be hard to justify spending hundreds, if not thousands, of dollars on classes. Even if money and time are not issues, it may be a long time since you've set foot in a classroom. You may feel funny going. I had to go to a training class for work. It was eight hours a day for two weeks in a city far from my home. I had to stay in the training facility's housing, and the other students were mostly a lot younger than I was. It was not a comfortable situation, and if another format were available, I would have chosen it.

When you are starting your learning journey, being uncomfortable can stall your progress. The good news is that the availability of classes today has expanded greatly due to technology. These classes range from YouTube videos to more organized videos on educational sites. There are also instructor-led classes online, so you get the benefit of having a teacher you can ask questions. These classes offer the benefit of being accessible from the comfort of your own home. Many don't require you to show yourself on the screen.

My go-to source for free classes is internet videos. These videos range from tutorials on how to fix a toilet to lectures on advanced economics. I find these classes to be very helpful. Since they are recorded, you cannot ask the teacher a question, but you can rewind and watch the video as many times as you need to understand it. These classes are also convenient. You can watch them on the train on your way to work, or late at night when you have some "me time." You can watch it for ten minutes, save it, and then finish it later. These classes are extremely flexible, and many are comprehensive. I want to put a drop ceiling in my basement. I found a 1-hour and 10-minute video on how to do it. I skimmed through it, liked what I saw, and saved it until I'm ready to do the work and need to learn how to do it.

These video classes are not perfect. They are missing some benefits that other classes offer. As I mentioned before, there is no teacher interaction, so you can't drill down to certain specifics. Video classes provide no student interaction. In a classroom, we tend to learn as much from other students as we do from the teacher, and there is also a networking opportunity, but these video classes are valuable as well. You do learn new things, and they can be a great way to reinvigorate your learning prowess. Using these videos can increase your confidence, so when you're ready to take the next step, your mind is in a learning mode.

Video content is not the only source on the internet. There are sites (some free, many for a fee) that give you access to teachers online, and many of these classes have some student interaction as well. If we can say that there was a benefit from the pandemic, it was the explosion of opportunities for video communication online. With the isolation the pandemic brought, we adapted and started getting more comfortable with online video communication. We can video chat with friends from across the nation or with business partners around the world. The face-to-face meeting has become a secondary means of communication. This communication shift has translated to the education sector. There are classes online that are led by teachers and that allow students to interact online. I have given online classes with student interaction in Singapore, India, and Saudi Arabia from my home office. Students were able to ask questions and interact with each other. Online classes have evolved into effective learning opportunities.

Colleges and other organizations offer these classes. Some of these offerings are local, and others are worldwide, so you can select the range of students you want to encounter. The prices can be lower than traditional college courses, and you have the opportunity to take the classes from home. These sources can give you access to schools outside of your area or just give you the convenience of learning from home. Some of the local ones will have student get-togethers so you can interact with the students offline.

These classes give you the professional teacher interaction that videos and books can't offer. There is value in being able to ask a teacher a question and have them rephrase a concept in a way that makes it more understandable for you. Having a teacher can be especially important if you are taking a class that you have no background in. These classes can be a great way of supplementing your education.

Online classes have not made traditional brick-and-mortar classroom-style schools obsolete. There are still a variety of learning opportunities available, ranging from for-profit courses provided by training companies to community-provided classes and classes offered by colleges/universities. With so many options available, there is no excuse not to take some kind of classes. Many companies will even cover the cost of the classes.

There are free classes in a classroom setting. You need to be a little more careful with this type. Many times, these classes are a means to sell you a product. You can glean information from those types of classes, but those are not the type of class I am recommending. Some organizations provide free education. Banks, for instance, are required to support the communities in which they work. One of the ways they do that is to offer classes to the community for free. There are a lot of organizations that offer job-hunting classes for free, and certain clubs offer training in the skillset that they represent.

It takes a little research, but with our good friend Google (or Bing, if you prefer), you can find a lot of free courses on many subjects. These classes are helpful and have valuable information, but to get a whole classroom experience, you will need to pay. There are also some very valuable web sources that cost money. These sources can help you advance to the next step, whether you've exhausted the free content, are seeking more interaction on a broader range of subjects or require accreditation to move forward.

There are organizations that offer training classes that last from an afternoon to a week. These classes are typically designed to provide career support. If you are looking at these classes, you should talk to your company. Even companies that don't have an official education system will allow you to participate in classes and may even pay for a part or all of the class. Taking classes like this helps you in three ways:

- § You get the skills in the class.
- § You get to network.
- § You signal to your employer that you want to learn—remember your Performance Image!

One of the most effective learning opportunities I have ever experienced is one you may have never heard of: the informational interview. An informational interview is a conversation with someone who has experience in the subject matter you want to learn about.

Have you ever started a job with a training class only to get out of the class to have people tell you the "real way" the work is done? There is not always a direct translation from the classroom to reality. There are certain things that are left out of the class because they are too specific, hard to explain, or controversial. Most people need experience to learn these hidden items, but you can learn these things through an informational interview.

It helps to have some base information before you set up the interview. If you go into the interview with very little information, you will end up using the time to get information you could get through other means. To be most effective, do some research first. Read about it, maybe take a class. Get enough information about the topic for you to speak intelligently about it and ask intelligent questions.

Now that you have your base information, what's missing? What information do you need to supplement what you have already learned? I was helping a recent college graduate with job hunting. She was a criminal justice major, but after some experience, she decided that she did not want to work directly with criminals. When talking about what she liked, she focused on investigations. She liked to investigate. She started to look into fraud and compliance investigations at banks as a potential career. She researched the laws and rules but lacked a clear understanding of what a compliance officer's daily responsibilities were or how to secure such a job. To address this, she arranged an informational interview. Through a networking partner, she arranged a meeting with the vice president of a local bank. The vice president invited the bank's experts to the meeting, and our graduate learned what it took and how to get onto a job track that would lead to that career.

The information she received is not available in a book or in a class. The informational interview gave her an inside view of what the job entails, so she could decide whether to pursue that career. She also learned the steps she needed to take if she wanted to pursue that job. She also improved her Performance Image. By arranging the interview and being prepared for it, she signaled to the bank VP that she is proactive, professional, and an out-of-the-box thinker. An informational interview will allow you to leapfrog your peers because you will have information that typically takes years of experience to gain.

Not everyone is a good candidate for an informational interview. Successful people are busy and don't necessarily have time to spare. There is also a large group of people who have plenty of time to talk but not much to say. It's your responsibility to tell the difference. You want to talk to the person who can give you the information you need, not someone who is talking to you because they have nothing else to do. The best way to identify these people is through networking.

Once you've gathered as much information as possible through traditional means and still need more, it's time to schedule an informational interview. Analyze the information you have and look for holes in it. Develop questions that will help you fill those holes. Once you have done that, talk with people in your network to find people who can help you. This may take several attempts. As mentioned before, successful people are busy and may not have time for you or may not see the value in meeting with you. Don't be discouraged. People saying no is part of the process. Be prepared for your interview and practice active listening and taking notes. This is not just for you. You are signaling to the interviewer that you are benefiting from the meeting, and the person won't feel like they are wasting their time.

Let's say that you benefit from an informational interview, and you want more. There is a next step that you can benefit from. The mentor/protégé relationship is not a new concept, but it is not used as much as it used to be. A mentor/protégé relationship can propel you forward like no other form of education.

There is nothing like real-world experience to help you learn the ropes. A mentor is a person who shares their experience to help you traverse the maze that is your life. There are pitfalls everywhere. If you can avoid those pitfalls, you can be more successful more quickly. Like the informational interview, this relationship starts with a conversation. You get information from your interviewee, and they see something in you that they want to invest in. The keyword here is relationship. The mentor/protégé relationship develops over time. You end up learning from and supporting each other as you grow as individuals.

Also, you don't need to be a young person to have a mentor. Your mentor does not even need to be older than you. People get experience at different rates. Do not let your ego get in the way when trying to acquire information. Technology is a good example. You may find someone half your age who can show you how to use technology more effectively. Don't pass up that opportunity just because you feel you are superior to the younger person because of the number of your years of experience compared to theirs.

Finding a mentor starts with your network. Consider all the people you know and apply the characteristics you are looking for to the list.

§   Do they have the experience you are looking for?

§   Do you feel comfortable sharing information with them?

§   Are they trustworthy?

Once you identify the person, ask them questions. Start off slowly and don't waste their time. Take an interest in them and encourage them to take an interest in you through your questions. Not every relationship will turn into a mentor relationship, so you will need to do it over again until you find the right person. Not everyone will have the time or communication skills to meet your needs. It may be that they don't feel comfortable with you. Don't push a relationship that is not working. Keep the person as a network contact and work with others until you find the mentor that works for you.

I have personally benefited from the mentor/protégé relationship from both sides. I have a mentor whom I've been meeting with on and off for the last thirty years. These days, we typically check in on each other a few times a year, but we still discuss issues that need to be resolved. He is in his eighties and still going strong. Even though we don't meet regularly, I still find inspiration from him, and I follow his example as I continue my personal development.

You can also benefit from being a mentor. From the people I mentor, I get access to potential employees and vendors. I also get a new perspective on how people see things differently than I do. It helps me to open my mind to new ideas and stay engaged with changes, rather than being left behind.

WHY

We mentioned that you can start slowly, but we have covered a lot of learning sources, and it can look like a lot of work. You may be asking yourself if it is worth your investment of time and money. It is much easier to watch TV than to take a college course, which is why most people sit in front of the TV.

Learning is the key to growth and maintaining flexibility. You gain experience faster, and you get the tools you need to succeed in places where you have limited experience. Learning is not easy. If you are not growing, you are dying. Water that lies undisturbed goes stagnant. Air in a closed space gets musty, and a mind that is not learning atrophies. Learning is a skill. It is about adapting to new environments or situations. Like any skill, if you do not practice it, you do not get better at it. You potentially start to lose the skill. Starting to learn again is like riding a bike. You can get back on the bike and start riding. That does not mean you start at the level where you left off. If you rode a bike competitively when you were younger and you stopped for twenty years, it will take time to rebuild your competency.

The same goes for learning. If the last time you took a class was in college twenty years ago, you may need some preparation to be able to thrive in the new training program your company wants to put you through.

HOW

How bad do you want to achieve An Authentic Success? There is a motivational speaker who talks about the importance of wanting to succeed. To paraphrase one of his stories, a student tells his teacher that he wants to succeed. The teacher takes him to the beach. He tells the student to walk out into the water. When they are up to their necks in the water, the student asks what this has to do with success. The teacher trips the student and holds him under the water until the student starts to struggle. When the student comes to the surface sputtering, the teacher says, "You need to want to succeed as much as you want to breathe."

Take the time and discipline yourself. Set aside twenty minutes every day to read. As mentioned above, it does not need to be some heavy tome on philosophy. Reading any book will help you. I recommend that you do at least some of your reading when you wake up in the morning. If you wait until bedtime every day, you will find that you only get in a few minutes a day before you fall asleep. Also, it is ok to read a couple of books at once. You may spend ten minutes every morning reading a book that teaches you a skill and then spend twenty minutes a night reading fiction. You can also listen to books in your car while you commute. I do this, and when I had a two-hour commute (each way), the books kept me sane.

If you have not been in a learning environment for a while, start small with classes. Watch some free online videos on a topic in which you are interested. Many of the videos are arranged in ten-minute to half-hour bite sizes, so you do not need to commit half your day to learning. Once you put your learning hat back on, expand to longer classes until you reach a point where you are comfortable with learning again. It can take a while. Learning is a skill, just like riding a bike, and it can take a while to knock the rust off. Once you get more proficient, you can expand your learning opportunities without increasing your time commitment too much.

Learning also gives you confidence. As an Authentic Achiever, you have seen your share of discouragement and setbacks. You have run up the hill only to slide back down. The knowledge and experience you gain from education are like a rope to help you climb that hill. It gives you the confidence to climb steeper hills and to break out of the Frustration Energy Cycle to get an Intentionally Sharpened Mind.

Reflection

Are you open to learning new things?
What are you willing to do to start your learning journey?
What is holding you back?

Goals

Document what you are willing to do to start your learning journey.

Actions

Start your learning journey today.

CHAPTER 7

The Technology Advantage

"All progress takes place outside the comfort zone."
–Michael John Bobak

*"The first step toward success is taken
when you refuse to be a captive of the environment
in which you first find yourself."*
–Mark Caine

The speed of technological advancement is so embedded in our thinking that it has become cliché. How are you responding to these advancements? Are you letting them pass you by, or are you embracing change and keeping up? If you think you are too old to learn new tech or that your life won't be affected, you risk being left behind. Like that cassette tape that has been sitting in a drawer for longer than you can remember, you can find yourself becoming obsolete.

Having to worry about becoming obsolete is a relatively new phenomenon. Before the technology spike that improved the ability to measure productivity, people were able to basically hide for their entire career. Come in late, do the minimum, go home on time, get their annual raise, and keep going. None of us can afford to do this anymore. Technological innovation has changed all of that. We need to succeed more effectively, and we don't have the luxury of wallowing in mediocrity and expecting no consequences.

We see this every day. At the grocery store, we have gone from cashiers to self-checkout, and now stores are experimenting with carts that record what you put in them so they can check you out automatically when you are done. What happens to the cashiers? I had to fly for business recently. I left from a smaller airport where I needed to speak with an agent to check my bag. On the return flight, I was able to do it at a kiosk and not talk to anyone. The kiosk was easier. What happens to the check-in agent?

Technology has gone from a tool to make you more efficient to a tool with the potential to replace you. Artificial intelligence (AI) has the potential to change the workforce more than the Industrial Revolution. I use AI constantly. Some examples include:

§   As a copywriter, when I develop advertisements

§   As an intern, when I need research done or a technical paper summarized

§   As an analyst, when I need a spreadsheet designed

I also use the internet to find overseas vendors to complete work for me at a fraction of the cost it would cost me locally. Using these tools helps me succeed faster and less expensively. The people who are being replaced need to adapt to stay relevant and competitive. How are you coping with the changes?

One of the top age stereotypes is discomfort with new technology. There is a common perception that young people are ready to embrace new technology, and older people tend to ignore it. The perception is common because it is based on truth. Tasks like paying bills online can cause discomfort for older adults. The inertia of mailing in payments and previous internet security issues can make people uncomfortable with a change to using technology. In general, younger people tend to be more tech-savvy and are quicker to embrace new technologies. The reluctance of older demographics is part of the two-edged sword of experience. If you have been writing checks for decades, you may be affected by inertia that hinders you from stopping to consider whether that skill continues to be the most effective. I fell into this trap with my banking. My daughter uses remote deposit capture, and I was still going to the branch to deposit checks. Finally, I had to stay at the house to meet a contractor, but I had several checks to deposit. I finally signed up for remote deposit capture and deposited my checks with my phone. It is convenient, quick, and safe. It made me much more efficient.

Resistance to change is natural. You have worked hard to get the experience you've earned, and you cherish it. You did not ask for all of this technology, and you've gotten along without it so far; why should you learn the new technology? The new technology will help you be more effective and can make your life easier.

If you have ignored technology, you are not alone. I work with a lot of finance people, and I am amazed at how many have very little exposure to MS Excel. Instead of utilizing the tools, they manually do stratifications and analyses. It takes them hours to do what I can in a few minutes because I have taken the time to learn the tool. They are stressed out to meet deadlines, but I have done it, submitted it, and have moved on to something else. Technology has made life easier.

If you have not embraced technology, you may feel forced to use it. For example, people may find themselves looking for a job after 20 years with an employer. Job postings are exclusively online. There are skills involved in completing effective online searches. If you have not done that, you can find yourself stumbling through the process and getting frustrated. Even though they are frustrated, many people don't take the time to learn the skills because of the inertia they have built over time.

People wander into technology because it replaces what they had, but do not embrace it or take the time to understand how to use it effectively. If you are caught up in this anti-technology inertia, you may get left behind. If other people learn the technology faster and can be more productive or even just have the appearance of knowing more than you, you are put at a disadvantage. The appearance of ignorance is bad, but especially so for the older person. If you have been around the block and you avoid technology, you are fulfilling the age stereotype of being behind the times. Technology is a tool; it is not a replacement for experience. Knowing how to use a tool is good. Having experience and knowing how to use a tool is better. I heard a story that demonstrates the point. A shipowner had a problem with one of his engines in his most productive ships. He was losing money every day, and the ship was not operational. He spent thousands of dollars with multiple mechanics to no avail. Finally, he hired an older, very experienced mechanic. Being frustrated over the lack of progress from previous attempts, the owner watched the old man work. The old man looked the whole engine over; he poked at it and prodded it, and finally, he went to his toolbox. He pulled out a small hammer and hit the engine in a specific spot. He then went to start the engine, and it worked.

The owner was very happy. A week later, the owner got a bill for $10,000. Having seen the man just hit the engine with a hammer, he asked for an itemized bill. The old man sent an itemized bill.

§   Hitting the engine with a hammer $10.00

§   Knowing where to hit it $9990.00

Having a tool does not mean a person knows how to use it effectively. You can offer tremendous value by leveraging your experience while using the most effective technology. The more you understand technology, the bigger your toolbox is. That knowledge also signals to your employer that you are aware of the technology and can offer more value than someone without your experience.

On the other hand, don't treat technology as the next shiny thing to look at by getting distracted by all of the technological noise out there. Research technology with the purpose of using it to make your life better. I was able to do this with Artificial Intelligence. There is a lot of content on the technology of AI. Many business-oriented presenters talk about the technology behind AI, but I am not in the technology industry. I don't need to know how AI works. I need to know how AI works for me. I am fortunate that one of my business coaches has taken the time to understand how AI can enhance efficiency. I have taken advantage of his presentations to learn how to use AI as a businessperson rather than learning how AI programming works behind the scenes.

Because of my experience and new skills with AI, I can perform question engineering effectively, converse with my AI tools, and develop solutions more quickly with fewer human resources. Question engineering is the development of specific questions formatted in a way that the AI understands it and gives you the results you need. The more complex the operation, the more detail is needed in the question.

It is important to know how to use your tools. Just like you would rather use a screwdriver than a hammer to drive in a screw, you want to use the right tool for your job. Just remember that sometimes the power screwdriver is too big for the space, and your experience getting a manual screwdriver up and behind a part that you can't see well is your best solution. If your only experience is technology, you might be lost when that technology fails you. When you realize that the technology is just one of the tools in your toolbox and your base experience provides you with other tools, you will get farther.

Using tools is a balancing act. If you have the experience but not the technology, you are doing the equivalent of hammering nails with a rock rather than a hammer. If you lack the experience but have the technology, it can be compared to a monkey with a hammer. Knowing the process is more important than knowing the technology, but knowing both puts you ahead of the people who just have one of those things. Efficient work does not come from just knowing about and understanding technology; it comes from leveraging both your experience and technology to get quality work done faster. If you understand what a hammer is and how to use it, but you still use a rock to hammer a nail, you are still not efficient. You can find more success by keeping up with and using technology to magnify your experience.

Technology comes in many forms. One of the most common is the App. These applications do a variety of tasks and are most commonly used on your smartphone. There are so many apps out there to help you with your day. There are calendaring and to-do list apps to keep you on track. There are mapping apps that help you get to where you want to go, whether you are driving in the suburbs or walking in the city. There are apps to help you find restaurants when you are traveling. There are a lot of apps that can save you time and money and just make life more interesting for you. These tools can help you leverage your skills and get you to the next level.

Apps can serve as tools or distractions. Companies know how to engage users and keep them engaged, even when the activity is not helping them achieve their goals. You need to take the time to determine which apps are helping you achieve your goals, and which apps are just distractions. Completely setting up a LinkedIn page can help you reach your goals. On the other hand, playing games on your phone probably won't help you reach your goals. Signing up for or writing blogs about your interests is helpful; mindlessly watching videos about people's pets probably isn't.

You don't need to be on the cutting edge. Getting the latest and greatest gadgets can be expensive, and not all technology has staying power. It helps to stay just ahead of the pack and know how to use the tools you have. If you have the super-duper phone with the watch that is connected, and all you do is take phone calls, that might be a waste. If you have a standard phone and you can map your way to an appointment, find a good restaurant for lunch, track your appointments, and your to-do list, you are ahead of the game.

The key is using the technology you have to the fullest. If you don't have much ancillary income, there are a lot of free options out there. If you can afford it, use the tools that best fit your needs. It helps to do some research to see which ones work best for you; then use them. You will not reach your goals by playing games on your phone. You can go further by being engaged and deliberate in your use of technology. You can make your life more efficient, so you get more done with the time you have. Every minute you save can be a minute you spend on your goals or leisure. It is important to remember that leisure is not a waste of time. Use your technology effectively, and you will be better equipped to achieve your goals.

Building Your Tech Toolbox

If you're not tech-savvy or just looking to get more engaged, there are ways to get on top of your game with technology. Because technology changes so quickly, I am not going to provide product names; I will just provide types.

§ Artificial Intelligence: AI has the potential to impact your life more than any other technology out there. It can make you more productive and has the potential to make many professions obsolete. If you do not learn how AI can make you more effective, you risk being left behind.

§ Centralized Productivity Enhancers: From calendaring apps to to-do lists. There is technology available that can help you stay on track and measure your progress. These apps can work on your phone and computer, so you can access them from anywhere, and you always know where you stand.

§ Business Process Tools: From word processing to spreadsheets and slide software, knowing your tools will help you be more efficient. These products offer many tools to make you more efficient. Leverage the tools you have, understand how they work, and how they can make your life easier.

§ Data Storage: Can you access your documents from your phone? There are data storage products that let you access your files from anywhere. Which is more professional: I'll send you that document now, or I'll be back to my office tomorrow and will get it to you then? If your competition gets the information to the client today, you are at a disadvantage.

§ Grammar Checking: We type fast and may not be as proficient typing on our phones. Having a spelling and grammar tool can save you from embarrassing misspellings and autocorrects. Some business process tools offer spelling/grammar tools, but I find some stand-alone products to be superior.

§ Presentations/Online Communication Tools: How many times have you heard someone say you're on mute? When people stumble on the mute button or on sharing a document in an online meeting, they look technologically inept. If this is you, you can lose credibility before you even speak. Understand how to use your tools and maintain situational awareness of your muting and video settings.

You can refer back to the Intentionally Sharpened Mind for ways to learn about technology. Technology is just another topic. There are a lot of learning resources out there to help you on your journey. Once you start to master AI, you will be able to use it to help you research topics, find sources of information, and organize them in a way that fits your learning style.

Even though you don't need to buy all the new tech gadgets, it helps to keep up with all the trends. It is important to know what is happening in the tech world and how it will affect you and your industry. Your job may count on it. If you were a gas lamp lighter as electric lights were introduced or a buggy whip maker when automobiles became affordable, you most likely found yourself out of a job. In England, there were riots when thousands of needle makers who crafted sewing needles and pins by hand were put out of business by automation. The needle makers were not ready for technological change, and their lifelong skills were made obsolete. You do not want to be obsolete. Take the time to keep on top of technology. Just to reiterate, AI has the potential to change the workplace as much as the Industrial Revolution. If you are not prepared and your workplace changes dramatically, you might find yourself with obsolete skills and no time to catch up.

Technology has also opened the employment marketplace to the world. Jobs that had to be local are now being fulfilled by vendors in the far corners of the world. The first experience of job export workers faced was in manufacturing. Shipping technology has enabled manufacturing to shift to lower-cost labor markets around the world, materially affecting workers in high-cost areas. Supply chain issues and customer preferences have brought some reversals, but it is still a factor. Cheaper labor combined with the technological advancements in some countries, along with technical advancements in transportation and logistics, allows for the mass importation of goods and now services. This phenomenon is now impacting the service industries. Call centers are now overseas. Chat functions when not operated by AI are also manned overseas. With internet-based phone systems, companies can now have people in other countries perform call center jobs. Initially, there was a backlash due to language barriers, but these barriers are being overcome through training. Even the automated switchboard has improved. Since voice recognition has improved, you don't see people yelling "YES!" into their phones as much. Technological developments have dramatically changed the employment landscape and have altered the types of opportunities available.

There are also websites that facilitate service transactions around the world. Anyone can hire virtual assistants, graphic designers, writers, researchers, and many other tasks from vendors worldwide from your computer. That can help people get cheaper services, but it also impacts the traditional providers. Everyone needs to adapt to keep up with these changes.

These technological advances typically add value. They reduce costs for companies and customers, make processes more efficient, and help improve poverty in other countries. These positive market improvements can have negative personal and local economic impact. If you were the call center manager who lost his job because the company moved, you experienced a materially negative impact on your career that can be difficult to recover from. Even if you did not lose your job, the additional competition reduces your chances for career growth. It is important to understand the potential impact of technical advances to protect yourself from loss and prepare yourself for the new opportunities. The threat is not just cheap labor elsewhere. The potential threats to your career lurk in technological advances in transportation to get the products from the countries in which they are produced to the stores in your neighborhood, or the internet phone to bring the representative from halfway around the world to your phone. Getting ahead of the changes puts you in a better position to succeed.

We have been looking at the risks of being left behind, but there are also tremendous opportunities for people who embrace technology. Change is not all negative. Technical advances can also create jobs. The same technologies that provide opportunities to others can offer them to you. I have been able to train people in Asia and the Middle East because of video conferencing. That technology allowed me to network with potential clients and deliver the training. I would not have been exposed to those opportunities without the new technology. The opportunities to offer freelance work can be an excellent opportunity to have a side gig. There are websites that help you get introduced to customers and handle payment collection.

Changes can drive innovation. Companies want to reduce costs and increase efficiency. This desire fuels technological innovation. If you can stay on top of technological changes in your industry, you will be prepared to succeed instead of being left behind.

It's important to keep an eye on technological trends to see how they can impact your life. It does not matter what line of work you are in. If you are in security, you can be impacted by drones. If you are in health services, you could be impacted by computerized record-keeping, automated health devices, and even artificial intelligence. If you are in the fast-food industry, you can be impacted by automated ordering kiosks. The list goes on and on. The travel agent industry was hit hard by internet travel service providers. Even garbage collection has been affected by technology. There used to be three guys and a truck. Now there is one guy with a robotic arm on the truck. An industry that looks like it will be materially impacted by automation is the Maritime Ports Industry. Unions are fighting the introduction of automation, but that will be a losing battle. People in that industry who embrace technology will be more likely to succeed as changes are implemented.

Even if your job or home life is not directly affected, knowing about technology is important. It keeps you relevant and signals to the people around you that you can add value in a changing environment. A common joke is about older people relying on the grandkids as IT support. If you are older, stereotypes project that you are not expected to understand new technology. If you do have an up-to-date understanding, you can add more value, preserve your relevance, and improve your Performance Image. You can leverage your experience and use your knowledge of what is coming to be more strategic. Your experience can allow you to accomplish more using technology and find new levels of success.

If you can avoid becoming a modern version of a gas lamp lighter, you will find yourself more able to succeed. If you see technology that will have an impact on your life, positive or negative, it helps to get out in front of it, so you can have more control of its impact on you, and you have a better chance of coming out on top. Embrace technology. It is coming whether you like it or not. You will be more successful if you can achieve a Technology Advantage.

Reflection

How comfortable are you with technology?
How would you describe your current usage of technology?
What are you willing to do to stay ahead of technology?

Goals

Determine what tech tools you have and what you can get to make you more efficient.

Actions

Develop a plan to leverage technology more effectively.

Using Your
Success Toolbox

CHAPTER 8

Position Yourself for Opportunity

"The starting point of all achievement is desire."
—**Napoleon Hill**

*"Logic will get you from A to B.
Imagination will take you everywhere."*
—**Albert Einstein**

You have probably heard that you must be in the right place at the right time to be successful. I believe that this is partially true. Showing up is 80 percent of success. Like the lottery advertisement says, "You can't win if you don't play." In the same way, it is harder to succeed if you are not prepared. If you have been implementing the ideas in this book so far, you are better prepared to achieve an Authentic Success. Preparation alone will not get you the success you desire. An Authentic Success requires engagement in the process.

One of the keys to engagement is awareness. You would be well served by being aware of what is going on around you and aware of trends that impact your life. In the chapter, The Technology Advantage, we discussed that you need to be aware of technological changes. Technology is only one facet of your environment that you may want to track. Do you know what is happening in your industry right now and how it can impact your success? If you are in the mortgage industry and rates are going up, which causes refinances to decrease; you can no longer rely on refinances as you once did. What can you now do to succeed? You are a tool maker at a helicopter plant, and there are cuts to the defense budget. What do you need to do to be successful? It can be like playing a game of chess. You need to think two or three moves ahead.

It is not only industry trends. How will inflation impact your lifestyle? As we saw in the pandemic, new pathogens can turn your world upside down. When was the last time you went to the doctor? A health issue can impact your life. Are there factors that are impacting your loved ones that can impact your life?

If you want to strategically stay current on trends that can impact your life, you can leverage some of the activities discussed in "The Intentionally Sharpened Mind" chapter, such as reading, learning, building mentor relationships, and using technology.

Using these activities can give you situational awareness. I first learned about situational awareness through my martial arts training. In martial arts, I was taught to keep an eye on my environment as part of my self-defense strategy. Situational awareness is not a paranoid looking-over-your-shoulder strategy. There are signs you can keep an eye out for that signal you should leave an area. You can use a similar strategy to traverse an uncertain environment in your life. Situational awareness helps you reach the goals you set for yourself while avoiding pitfalls.

Situational awareness is basically knowing what is happening around you at any time. Using the self-defense analogy, being engrossed in your cell phone while you are walking through a dark parking lot can distract you to the point that you miss signs and walk into a dangerous situation. In a similar way, if you are employed in a volatile industry in an uncertain environment and are relying on your past success to guide your next steps, you may find yourself struggling and trying to catch up when you have a setback.

Continuing the self-defense analogy, if you are walking down the street and you see a group of teenagers harassing people as they walk, what do you do? Do you walk into them, or do you find a way to avoid them? The same goes for your career. If you hear rumblings that your job is at risk of being outsourced or that your company is buying technology that has the potential of making your position obsolete, what do you do? Do you keep doing what you have been doing, or do you make changes to reduce your risks?

It is always better to have an idea of what is coming so you can react to it. Unfortunately, we do not have crystal balls to tell us the future. We need to make educated guesses on what to do next. This means leveraging our experience. It helps to be nimble. Being nimble means, we need to have the pragmatism and energy to try new strategies. You probably have to work with other people. Life is generally a team sport. It is difficult to go it alone and expect to achieve your full potential. Success is also a numbers game. Situational awareness techniques can expand the environment you are monitoring. You can look for signs of change in many areas that have the potential to impact you. One way to broaden your awareness is to build your network beyond your immediate environment.

As discussed, the path to achieving bigger goals is to add more value by doing more things. Doing more requires change. Doing things the way they have always been done is the kiss of death for an Authentic Achiever. Circumstances change faster now than they ever have in the past. Technology changes, jobs migrate, productivity increases, and industries are born and die. The only constant is change. If you do not move with the change, you will be left behind. It is important to keep an open mind to change, to change when it is appropriate, and to embrace positive change.

Changing for the sake of change is not the answer either. Following fads will just wear you down and will not get you to where you need to go. It is a challenging balancing act. Having an open mind means that you will thoughtfully embrace change, not throw everything away and start again each time a new fad comes out. You need to leverage your experience and embrace change to find the correct path.

If you don't know what the changes are, you cannot embrace the change. You will find yourself being dragged along, willingly or not, by those who are informed of changes. You probably have experienced this if you work for a larger company. All of a sudden, there is a new initiative for productivity or morale, or respect in the workplace. These changes can seem to come out of nowhere and often do not seem to make sense.

As we position ourselves for success, it is time to start bringing everything we learned together and building our plan. Working hard and keeping your nose to the grindstone is no longer the strategy for success. It helps to be versed in the innovations that will impact your life. and to think about solutions before you need them. If you can get to the point where you have an idea of what is going to happen and have a set of recommendations, you will have added more value than you do now.

Part of open-mindedness is flexibility, and flexibility is applicable in both physical and mental ways. To maintain youthful energy, you need to be flexible in mind and body. Being mobile is just as important as being mentally sharp in maintaining energy.

It helps to be able to adapt and thrive in an environment of constantly moving targets and be pragmatic and flexible. If you get set in your ways and try to bull your way through life, you will get a lot of resistance and have trouble succeeding. Flexibility, however, does not mean just going with the flow. You can blaze your own path while reading the signs and adjusting your plans to meet your goals.

It is a fine line to stay on your path to reach your goals while remaining flexible as your environment changes. Flexibility helps you get through the storm. Think of a tree on a hill. That tree has to be able to withstand the winds and stay rooted. You need to do the same. You stick to your goals and your values, you are rooted, but you are able to flex in the winds; otherwise, the winds will eventually break you. If you find yourself in constant storms, you may need a new environment. If your workplace is in a constant tornado, you will eventually lose your roots and will become ungrounded. But typically, storms come and go, so you can weather them.

The same flexibility can help you in your personal life. You have your values and personal goals, but the world is a constant whirlwind. You are buffeted by negative thoughts and ideas that violate your values. You are given choices that do not meet your needs, and your families are exposed to situations from which you want to protect them. By keeping your roots and letting the negativity flow past you, you can weather these negative forces and stay grounded.

Now that you understand your environment and are ready to withstand the changes, it is time to determine what you want to accomplish and find the keys to achieving those goals. Then you may want to think about the base skills and how you can apply them in unconventional ways to set you apart and help you succeed where others fail.

§   You are a teacher, and you have reached the kids. You may need to reach out to the parents to get them involved to get to the next level.

§   You are a manager. You want to get to the next level. Take on projects outside of your normal duties to show you have what it takes.

You'll notice that these value-add projects are visible in the way you want them to be visible. You are building a Performance Image. You are applying your experiences and enhancing them by gaining new knowledge and additional experience. Taking a class adds to your knowledge, but until you use this knowledge and it becomes visible, it adds no value to Performance Image. If you don't use the knowledge visibly, it does not help you to deliver your product to your consumers, whether those consumers are your boss, your kids, your spouse, or your friends. I'm not saying you should go to the extreme and start to think of life as transactional. We don't offer our families love in exchange for something, and we shouldn't begin to. Equating your actions as products makes it easier for you to improve them. If you see your love as a product that your family needs, it is easier for you to look at it objectively and improve it. For example, if you see that being more attentive to your family when you are home increases the quality of their lives, you can make changes that improve their lives without too much of a cost to your own life. Again, this is not transactional. This process helps you measure your performance so you can improve. Measuring your expression of feelings to the people around you can be difficult. Most of us are familiar with performance evaluations at work. Utilizing these familiar methods can help you improve performance in your personal life.

Delivering this extra value does have costs. Even being more engaged at home costs you the opportunity to complete other tasks. As we discussed in the Performance Image chapter, it takes energy to do extra work. You can't expect to achieve an Authentic Success if you don't have the energy to do the work. You can't be engaged in achieving your goals if you are too tired to even get out of bed. You can't drive your car forever without stopping for gas, and you can't expect to get more done if you do not increase your energy. To reach your Authentic Success, you need to do more, so you need strategies to increase your energy.

We talked about developing your Turbocharged Mindset. It is important to build and maintain your mindset because it will be under attack. Attacks will come from your environment, trying to knock you down. You may even find yourself sabotaging your own efforts. Even the most supportive environments have toxicities that will attack your mindset.

If negativity surrounds you, you have less of a chance to succeed. If you are surrounded by people who commiserate about being too old to do anything, you will start to feel the same way. When you get into your late forties and early fifties, you find that people you went to high school with are now grandparents, and some may have died. You may be a grandparent too. If you are like me, you picture grandparents being old, retired people, not people with goals still to achieve. That view can sabotage your performance if you end up projecting an image of a person past their prime on yourself. Just because some of your peers are grandparents or have passed away does not mean you are too old to accomplish goals.

If you surround yourself with people and things that try to convince you that you are not able to achieve your goals for any reason, you will have trouble overcoming them. No matter how strong your mindset is, if you are in a negative environment, it will drain your energy. It can be tiresome and depressing to be in a negative environment. If you are going to succeed, you need to make every effort to get out of that environment.

If you have a negative attitude, thinking that the world is against you, you will have trouble succeeding. It's best to have an attitude that you can and will succeed if you do the right things. You may not know what those things are yet, but you will succeed when you find them. Without an attitude that says you can succeed, you will not succeed. Your brain needs to be on board with your plan. When you have the right attitude and you are enthusiastic, that will build the energy you need.

Think back to a time when you were exhausted, then found you had the opportunity to do something you really wanted to do. What was your reaction?

§   Did you get a boost of energy, ready to go for it?

§   Did you feel even more tired because you are disappointed with feeling too tired?

You almost certainly felt the first when you were younger. You came home from a hard day at school, and you just wanted to go to your room. Then it is time to get ice cream. You are suddenly ready to get up and go. You may have felt the latter as you got older. You had a hard week at work, and you had the opportunity to see your favorite sport. Going to your favorite chair may seem like a better option.

These reactions are based on your mindset and energy level. You were tired, but you became untired when you got excited (or more tired). You have control over your mindset and energy levels, whether you know it or not. Your mindset can make the difference. This may not be an instant change. You may need to implement the changes discussed in the Performance Image to boost your energy levels, which can take time. However, your change in mindset will provide some results right away.

Life can be hard enough without you introducing negative influences into your life. The addition of a negative environment can suck you dry. These negative environments can attack us from all angles:

§   A toxic workplace

§   An activity group that ends up being a gossip session

§   A weekly poker game that ends up being a bitch session over stale complaints

Those environments can foster a negative attitude in you and become an energy drain that can keep you from achieving your goals. When I was unemployed, I went to job-hunting networking groups. Most were positive experiences. One was a discussion about the poor job market, how it was impossible for older workers to find employment, and other negative talk. There was a segment for people to talk about their accomplishments, and one participant talked about how he got a third interview with a company, but he was certain he wouldn't get the job. I never attended that meeting again. Job hunting is discouraging enough. Adding a negative environment to the mix only sabotages your progress.

If you allow outside forces to direct you, you can be pulled in directions you don't want to go. It is easy to get dragged along with the crowd. If you keep to your values and remain flexible, you can withstand the storm and get what you want without changing your values or compromising your goals. As an Authentic Achiever, you have been around a while and have seen things your younger peers have not. It is time to use that experience to achieve your goals.

As we have discussed, experience is a two-edged sword. It gives you the information you need to succeed, but it can also put you in a state of mind that makes you less flexible. It is easy to get into the "we have always done it that way" mentality. This is especially true for people who have been successful and rewarded at lower levels of an organization. You are trained to believe that certain actions are the path to success. Those traits are positive for people who stay in their current roles, but if you are moving up in the organization, those traits can hold you back.

An easy example is growth in a sales organization. You can be a top-notch salesperson but be an awful sales manager. The skills that make one a great salesperson do not necessarily translate well to sales management. If you want to move up in a sales organization, you can preserve the skills you learned as a successful salesperson but be flexible enough to learn the skills you need to be a sales manager. Some of the sales skills are transferable, but they are different enough that you need to be flexible.

If you are flexible, you will have less trouble adapting. Your experience as a salesperson gives you credibility with your new subordinates. Your sales skills will allow you to help your team members when they are struggling with a tough customer. You can go in and help close the sale. What are some skills you may need to learn?

§   **Coaching:** Keep your people motivated and effective

§   **Teaching:** Share your experience with others to scale your effectiveness

§   **Measuring:** Track and measure the effectiveness of your people and determine if the changes you make are effective

§   **Leadership:** Lead your group

§   **Collaboration:** You now have responsibilities beyond sales. How are you going to work with the leaders in other areas of the company?

If you are performing a project around the house, there are certain tools you need. I just installed a dishwasher in my kitchen. I opened the box, took out the instructions, sat down, and read them. The instructions told me what tools and parts I would need, so I gathered all those items and organized them accordingly. When I was putting in the dishwasher, I ran into some very frustrating situations. When I got frustrated, I took a step back and a deep breath. That cleared my head, and I was able to get back to work. The same things are needed in your life. You need to take an inventory of your skills and experience when you are starting a new project. If you lack some of the necessary skills, research and learn how to accomplish what needs to be done. When you hit rough spots, you need to step back, take a deep breath, and then get back to work.

To achieve an Authentic Success, you need to want it. Desire is what keeps you motivated. If you don't want success enough, you will find excuses to avoid the work you need to do to achieve your goals and may eventually give up. Bingeing on the new program on the streaming service will look better than reading the book on Excel. The couch will look better than the gym. The burger will look better than your weight loss. Your bed will look better than your lesson plans. Without a strong desire, you can't get through the obstacles. The excuses will win.

It helps to treat your desire to succeed as a living thing. Desire needs to be fed and nurtured. It needs to grow, or it will die. Think of your desire as a houseplant. You need to give it sunlight, water, and food. Otherwise, it will shrivel and die.

§   **Sunshine**: Look at your goal every day. Visualize your success and have it become part of you. If you are not visualizing your goal every day, it will fade.

§   **Water**: Nurture your goal. Make plans and follow through on those plans with micro goals to set a path to your goal.

§   **Feeding**: Learn more skills to help you turn your desire into reality.

Now that you have determined that you want something. What are you prepared to do to get it? Are you prepared to work for your goal? You need to translate your desire into action. If you do not take action, you will just be a dreamer. Rewards are rarely served on a silver platter. You need to go out and get them.

Taking action can be easier said than done. It is easier and more satisfying to get what you want now versus getting what you want most. In other words, it is easier to satiate the desire to have a donut now than it is to stick to an 18-month plan to get into shape. You have to really want to be in shape to decide against the instant gratification of the donut.

Action builds momentum. What works in physics works in goal achievement. An object that is in motion tends to stay in motion; an object at rest tends to stay at rest. This applies to our goal achievement as much as it does to a marble rolling down a slope. The more action you take, the easier it is to continue to take action. We have all heard things like "the guy is on a roll."

Once you get going, it is easier to keep going. Obstacles cause friction. When we encounter an obstacle, it's like putting on the brakes or running through mud. We can lose traction and lose our momentum. If we are not consistent with our actions, when we hit a pitfall, we are more likely to get stuck. If we are more consistent with our actions, we have a better chance of getting through the pitfall.

Weight loss is a good example of how actions can help you overcome obstacles. When we first start our weight loss journey, we're motivated and work out and eat right. Then we hit an obstacle. We have to go on a business trip. With a packed schedule, bad sleep in a lumpy hotel bed, and big dinners, we go off track with our routine. We fight to get back on the routine, then it's Joe's birthday. Cake for everyone in the office, and you want to look like a team player, so you join in. These obstacles keep coming.

Once you have a routine, it is easier. You start working out in the morning, so you get it done before you get distracted by everything that happens in your day. You plan your meals, so you are better able to stay on track. Your eating habits change, so you are not as tempted by the treats at work. You start to see results, and you start feeling rewarded. You are building momentum, and you are better able to overcome pitfalls because you have built momentum.

To reiterate, action is key to success. I wanted to write this book. Writing a book takes hours upon hours of work. How can a busy person fit more hours of work into their schedule? I did it by committing to writing at least ten minutes a day every day. I hit obstacles. At a conference, I was exhausted in the morning, so I sat there for ten minutes and managed to write about thirty words. Not every day will be productive. As I consistently worked at writing, I found that ten minutes turned into thirty minutes or longer. Some days I was on a roll and wrote 600 words in the time I allowed. Consistency helped me build momentum. I made a point to get up at 4:45 a.m. every morning so I can get my writing done before my family is awake, work, and the distractions life brings every day.

You have some decisions to make.

1.   What are you willing to do to achieve your goals?

2.   What time of day is the best time for you to work on those goals?

3.   Are you willing to be consistent in your actions?

Nothing gets done until you make the decision to do something.

As you are making these decisions, you may be wondering where you should start on your path to an Authentic Success. A good place to start is a reflection on your own experience. Your experience may only tell you that you have been on the wrong path, but that is a start. You have worked at building your life for many years. Whether you have been stuck in a destructive cycle, you have been going with the flow on a path to mediocrity, or you have been working toward big goals, your experience tells a story. If you listen to that story, you may find it gives you unexpected insights.

As we've discussed, reflection is crucial to make sure your success is not influenced by societal norms. Movies and American culture, in general, have idolized the money-makers. Whether they are business-people, actors, or athletes, success has been measured in money earned, not necessarily in the life lived. If money were the only criterion, then the founder of a successful charity could not be considered successful, because that person has not made as much money as a professional athlete.

You don't need to have high earnings to be an Authentic Success. Higher earnings can give you more options for success, but it is not a requirement. An Authentic Success is achieving goals as you define them. If a parent wants to give up material things to raise their children, they can be successful. If an executive is burnt out and starts a restaurant, they are on a path to success. I am not a person to say, "Just follow your passion". Chasing passions can be expensive and unfruitful without a feasible market. There is a Japanese concept called Ikigai, which means a reason for being. You often see it represented by a Venn Diagram with four circles:

1. What you love
2. What the world needs
3. What you can get paid for
4. What you are good at

At the intersection of these circles is your reason for being.

You'll notice that two of the circles are internal and two are external. You determine what success means to you, but you need to adapt it so it serves others and provides you with income. You do not live in isolation, and you need to earn a living. An Authentic Success is a holistic success, not goals achieved in isolation.

> **"Success? I don't know what that word means.
> I'm happy. But success, that goes back to what, in
> somebody's eyes, success means. For me, success is
> inner peace. That's a good day for me."**
> **–Denzel Washington**

Putting your tools to use on your journey to an Authentic Success is unique to you. Your experience is a personal thing. I cannot tell you what value your experience has provided you since I have not lived it. You are the only one who has lived your experience. You are the only one who understands it. Since your journey is unique to you, it's best to be cautious of people giving advice. People who freely give advice may only want to make themselves feel important, and they do not necessarily know your true potential. They have not lived the life that you lived, so if they do not include your feedback in their assessment, their advice may be flawed.

Many people will tell you your faults. It can seem like everyone wants to help you identify what you've done wrong and why you need to be cautious, avoiding the risks necessary to achieve Authentic Success. Don't look at mistakes as endpoints. They can provide the best lessons. As long as the mistake has taught you something, then you are ahead of the game, no matter what your critics say. If you touch a hot stove and burn yourself, you have learned a lesson better than any class can teach. It is up to you to use the lesson to maximize that experience to achieve your goals. If you continue to touch hot stoves and burn yourself, then you have not learned the lesson. On the flip side, if you never touch a cold stove again, you have still not learned the lesson. If you remember that a hot stove will burn you, but a cold stove will not, you have learned a lesson. You have an asset. You are better at managing the stove than you were before.

Your critics may come back to you and say that you are bad at managing the stove because you burned yourself. The opposite is actually true. You are a better manager of the stove. You have firsthand knowledge of what the stove can do, and you are in a better position to train others to use it. This may be a silly example, but it demonstrates how mistakes teach and how the lessons you learn will have an impact on your future success.

I am not saying you should go out and try to make mistakes. Mistakes can be costly lessons. In the Performance Image chapter, I told you about my sick day costing me the respect of the president of the company. The fact that I was actually sick did not matter. When I am responsible for a task, I am responsible. Not understanding the importance of that responsibility was a mistake that cost me years of progress. Whether I'm sick, stuck in an airport, or facing another challenge, I'm responsible and need to deliver. Even to this day (decades later), there are a couple of people who don't trust me as they did before that day. Does that mean I can never be sick or have any other problems? No, it means I need to leverage other resources to ensure the job gets done.

These examples of responses demonstrate the lesson I learned from that mistake. Which sounds more professional, "I am sorry, boss, I am sick and can't present at the client meeting in two hours," or" I am sorry, boss, I am sick, so I am having Marty present at the meeting today. He is prepared, and I am confident he will do a good job."

It would be better for me if I could make the presentation. I am missing an opportunity, but by providing a replacement for the meeting, I have fulfilled my responsibility and did not leave my boss in a bad spot.

It can be easy to miss that the sick day was a mistake. If you don't know it is a mistake, you can't learn from it. Being burned by a stove is an easy mistake to identify. Calling in sick when you have the flu may not be. It wasn't an easy lesson for me to see. It took time. As discussed before, I started getting passed over for key assignments, and it put me back a couple of years in my career development. I had to invest time reflecting on my experience to realize the mistake I had made. Reflection on your history is one of the ways your experience can help you learn and move forward more effectively.

The activities that bring you success and make you happy are also keys to use in finding your path. If you are an accountant but find helping people with their careers more satisfying, you may be better in human resources. If you are in corporate America but find more satisfaction in charity work, you may be better off working at a nonprofit. You need to review your experiences and use them to find a path to success. Whether that review finds that you are on the right or wrong path, you have built a wealth of assets from those experiences. The ideas you have had, the lessons you have learned, and the people you have met can all help you in your path. You need to review and document your experiences and leverage those assets as you move forward in the achievement of your goals.

I am an Authentic Achiever. I have been working towards my life goals for many years and finally feel that I am getting traction. It is a lot of hard work with long hours, time, and money invested, a bit of travel involved, and family and household responsibilities. I am always busy. I get up early, so I can do some of my reading and writing. Typically, I had written this book between 4:45 a.m. and 6:30 a.m. in the morning, depending on my schedule. Then I would put in a ten-hour day. I would work out when I could and do what had to be done around the house. From my experiments with pushing myself, I found that I needed to follow the activities in the Performance Image chapter to maintain my pace. Are you ready to put your toolbox to work? When opportunity knocks, it helps to be able to open the door. Suppose the job you wanted or any other opportunity you've always wanted to accomplish came to you, but you were ill-prepared to accomplish it. In that case, that might be worse than never seeing the opportunity in the first place. Opportunities rarely fall into our laps, and when they do, we need to take them.

Taking advantage of opportunities requires effective action, and effective action requires utilizing your toolbox. Many people either don't know that they have a toolbox or how to use it effectively, so those people sit on the sidelines rather than striving for an Authentic Success. Not understanding their potential is the primary reason why, after age thirty, or forty, or fifty, people give up their dreams. Typically, when people say they are too old for something, that means that they don't believe they have the potential, or they have accumulated anxiety and regret, causing them to lose the drive to work toward the goal.

Now, some things might be out of reach. It is unlikely that someone will be an Olympic sprinter at age fifty, but that person might complete an obstacle course race. As I mentioned earlier, I have had people younger than me tell me that they are too old to do what I do. The fact that I am older and do the task means the issue they are experiencing lies elsewhere. Why can't these people do what I do? It probably isn't that they can't. It is more likely that they won't. They are not as committed to success as I am. Are you willing to commit to your success?

We don't live in fantasy land. There will be some things you can't do. However, you will probably find that many of the "can't do" turn out to be "won't do." That is good news. If you won't do those tasks, that means you are making a choice. If you are making a choice, you have control. If you have control, then you can make changes. If you can make changes, you can get on the path to your goals. It takes discipline and hard work, but you can do it.

There is a reason most people give up on their dreams and settle into a routine. It is easier to give up. It is easy to watch TV and eat processed food. It is easy to go to the same boring job every day. It is hard to go out and achieve your goals. It is easy to settle into a mundane routine. The easy path ends in regrets and lost dreams. If you take the Authentic Success path, you can find that the hard work has the benefit of the satisfaction of reaching your goals.

Be ready for the opportunity. Start now to build the discipline to do the things we discussed in this book. Now that you have the energy and confidence, you need to get to where you want to go. Remember that you don't have to go alone. Now it is time to build your team, your Authentic Success Mastermind Group.

DEVELOPING YOUR AUTHENTIC SUCCESS MASTERMIND GROUP

The quote, "No man is an island," is very cliché, but it is true. It can be very hard to succeed on your own. You need people around you to grow, and it helps to have the right people around when you are scouting new opportunities. Many of us have the misconception that a mentor or sponsor is someone who gives you a job. There are very few people who will look at you and say, "We need this person in the organization, and we will pay them lots of money." It doesn't quite work that way, and mentors can exist outside the workplace as well as inside. Mentors are teachers and advisors, not the goose that laid the golden egg.

If you take one lesson from this book, I recommend that it is how to develop your Mastermind Group. We have talked about how you can use your experience to leverage your efforts to execute. Now it's time to see how we can multiply our efforts by integrating our experience with our team's experience.

Think back to a time you worked with others to achieve goals. Were you looking for help, or were you looking to collaborate with others? Were you looking for independent advice or validation of your actions? Were you looking for helpers or partners?

"Successful people are always looking for opportunities to help others. Unsuccessful people are always asking, 'What's in it for me?'"
–Brian Tracy

The Authentic Success Mastermind Group is a 360-degree network that completely surrounds you. It is comprised of mutually beneficial relationships at multiple levels and includes four general categories of team members.

1. **Sponsor:** The sponsor provides access to opportunities. The sponsor might be multiple people, like a customer base. It can also be a single executive who has a career move to offer.

2. **Mentor:** The mentor is a person with more experience than you who you can learn from and guide you on your path. You can have multiple mentors for different aspects of your life.

3. **Peers:** These are the people on the same level as you. They may have different careers, but they are generally at the same level.

4. **Subordinates:** These members don't have to be people who report to you. They are people who have less experience than you.

The best case is a team that includes all of these people. They each carry a specific perspective that can be valuable to you. There is a good chance that you have some or most of these people in your circle already. You may not have thought of them in these categories. By putting them in categories, you can determine how complete your team is. As you and your team grow, you'll find that some people will migrate between categories. You may see mentors change into sponsors. As you grow, you might find that sponsors become peers, and as subordinates grow, they may become peers. It is important to recognize when your team evolves so you can make the most of your team and offer them the support that they need.

This team can communicate different opportunities to you as you are searching, and they can help you take advantage of them. To reciprocate, you can find opportunities to assist your teammates.

§   You can fill the need of a sponsor, making their lives easier, and in return, you can have a satisfying career change.

§   A mentor might know a person with a need, and in return, you can fill it. You make it possible for a mentor to help a colleague, and you get a satisfying career move.

§   You need support in your next move, so you hire peers and subordinates or get them hired in other positions.

These are ways of getting your network to work for you. They see that you will help them. You are not just a taker. Remember that this is a team, not a group of service providers. Expect to help all of these people out as much, if not more than, they help you out. This team is not like a sports team. The members don't need to work together and may not even know each other. They are a team formed around you.

If you take and take and take, you are not a team member. You are a moocher. How many times have you gotten a call or an email from someone you have not talked to in years asking for help with a job search or some other thing? They never checked in to see how you were doing. They never offered help on anything. They just asked you for a job after years of no communication. How does that make you feel? If you're like me, you're not feeling good about it. Don't be that person. Your team is an asset that you need to nourish. Feed it if you want to harvest from it. It is just like a garden. If you nurture and cultivate it, you can have a rich harvest.

Take some time to reflect. What does your team look like right now?

§   Do you know the right people to help you reach your goals?

§   Do you have the sponsor, mentor, peer, and subordinate relationships?

It's okay if you don't or if they are not a great fit for you. Your team will ebb and flow over time. At times, you will have a well-staffed team, and at other times, your team will have weaknesses. At the time of this writing, I have a shortage of sponsors due to retirements and people slowing down. There have been times that I have had great sponsors, and I know how we can help each other, so I am on a search for new ones. A great method to find them is networking. Remember that networking is not a one-way street. Networking is about building relationships and helping people reach their goals.

GETTING GUIDANCE IS WORTH THE EFFORT

The mentor/protégé relationship is so valuable that it warrants a more detailed explanation. Many people don't see the value in a mentor-protégé relationship and find pursuing one a little daunting. The toughest obstacles you will face in building a relationship with a mentor are in your mind.

§   Feeling afraid of looking foolish or showing weakness

§   Not feel comfortable sharing your failings with others

§   Being stubborn and not wanting to follow the advice of others

§   Believing you are too old to have a mentor

These feelings can make people reluctant to enter into the mentor-protégé relationship.

I have several mentors. These are not formal "mentor" relationships, like some companies attempt to establish. These are relationships built over the years with people I respect. These are people younger than me, my age, and older than me. They have a wide range of experiences, and they can act as sounding boards when I have a problem, and they teach me stuff out of the blue. Most of the time, it's just talking. They are friendships with the benefit of access to expertise. In response, I am a good friend to them. I have helped them fill jobs, get customers, and sometimes offer my own advice. Always remember, the mentor relationship can be a two-way street. If the mentor can get as much out of it as the protégé, that is a solid relationship.

We discussed the negative impact of inertia, which comes from following a path over time, and how difficult it can be to overcome. Overcoming the inertia to put us in a position to achieve our goals can be like turning the Titanic. It can feel nearly impossible to do it on your own. That is why you shouldn't try to do it on your own. A mentor can guide you and give you the support you need to overcome inertia and get on a path to your Authentic Success.

There are moments in history when members of society were left behind. We may be in one of those times now with Artificial Intelligence and other technologies. Read about the introduction of pin-making machines in England during the Industrial Revolution, which we mentioned in the Technology Advantage Chapter, to see an extreme example of people being left behind. There is a good chance that people who stick to their path with no consideration for the changes around them can be left behind. If you have isolated yourself from the changes going on around you and have not built the proper relationships, you could be in trouble if the environment changes dramatically.

Having mentors can help you choose your path in a rapidly changing environment. You can also guide people. In martial arts, one of the final tools for learning is teaching others. When you have to teach others, it helps you gain a new understanding. The same goes for mentoring. When you mentor others, you find out more about yourself. There are other benefits to being a mentor. It will expose you to up-and-comers who can teach you the trends you need to keep an eye on to stay relevant. This connection becomes more important as we get older. We need to fight the tendency to sit back and disconnect. It is a battle for relevance. In my writing, I have used canoeing upriver as an analogy for fitness as we get older. If we stop paddling, the river pushes us back downstream. This analogy also fits our career and everything else we work hard for. We paddled upriver to be a good manager, or we paddled upriver to be a good teacher, or we paddle upriver to be a good martial artist.

Mentors can't paddle for you, but they can remind you why you are paddling in the first place. They can cheer you on when you are tired. They can tell you to steer to avoid the rapids. They can show you how to paddle more effectively, so it does not take as much effort. No matter how old you are, a coach or mentor will help you get to where you want to go faster than you could get there on your own.

As you network, you will find all kinds of people. Most will not qualify for your team. They may end up being great networking partners, but they may not have what you want to be on your team. You are not obligated to include anyone. Even though you are helping your team more than they help you at times, the purpose of your team is your growth. When you have exhausted your established network, it may be time to grow your network to find your team members. This work can be uncomfortable because you will be working at the periphery of your network with people you may not know well. The following strategies can help you develop your networking plan.

§ **Introductions:** I asked for introductions, targeted (specific people) and general (industry stakeholders my contact knew)

§ **Informational Interviews:** I spoke to industry stakeholders to gather information, conduct trend analyses, and obtain more introductions

§ **Attend Industry Events:** I attended conferences, seminars, and workshops in person and online and followed up with key stakeholders

§ **Leverage Social Media:** I hit LinkedIn hard and connected with professionals I wanted to meet

It is more comfortable to stay in your network's inner circle, but if you find it's not as productive as it once was, it might be time to expand it. Don't get angry with your network; develop and grow it so it better meets your needs.

To achieve an Authentic Success, you will need the support of other people, and to find those people, it helps to network. We have discussed networking throughout the book. Remember that networking is building relationships. Experiment in different places to network and take the time to talk to people. The more you do it, the better you will get at it. It may take a while to build the correct network. The people you need to know may be three degrees of separation from your current network. That means you need to navigate through three layers of people, showing that you are a productive network partner, to get to the people you need to know.

Networking is a lot of work, and it can be frustrating, which is why most people don't do it. That is also why we get the cries for help after ten years of silence when people lose their jobs. Having the right network has many benefits. You can hear about new information before your peers. You have access to job listings that most people don't. Not all those jobs are meant for you. Hearing about those jobs can help your network partners and team members succeed. You help someone fill an opening, and you get someone a job. You have helped two people with one action. You have shown yourself to have a valuable network and your willingness to use it to help others. These are valuable assets that can be used to get you what you need from your network, plus you get the satisfaction of helping friends out.

"It is literally true that you can succeed best and quickest by helping others to succeed." –Napoleon Hill

As I said before, a good network is like a garden. More than likely, you will find a lot of weeds in your garden. That is unavoidable. You need to control them so they don't overwhelm your fruit-bearing plants. You will find that certain unproductive people will try to take all your time. It is a trap that many networkers fall into. A good example comes from an experience I had at a conference with a coworker. We were trying to drum up business for our company. There were a couple of people there who could not add value to the company, and there was no strategic reason to talk to them. They ended up taking a couple of hours of my coworker's time that would have been better spent talking to other people.

Now you shouldn't be rude to these network weeds. Unlike the garden, network weeds can turn into fruit-bearing plants over time, but they can suck you dry right now. My coworker should have spent 15 minutes talking with them and then found a way to extricate himself from the conversation. He then would have had time to talk with people who could have had a more immediate impact on the company.

Whether you are at a conference or a happy hour, you should watch out for network weeds. Practice pulling out of conversations even if you have to say you need to go to the bathroom. When you are networking, every interaction you have with people should be strategic. Even if that just means that you don't want your happy hour monopolized by a boring blowhard. Sometimes you need to talk to the blowhard, but you should not feel obligated to do so. You may even want to be strategic in your recreation. Otherwise, you will be vulnerable to the whims of other people, and that happy hour can end up being a boring waste of time.

"If you don't design your own life plan, chances are you'll fall into someone else's plan. And guess what they have planned for you? Not much."
–Jim Rohn

Keep your network fresh and well-worked. Always add new people to it. Keep in touch with the other members, even if it is just to drop them a note on LinkedIn every few months. Go out and build the network that will help you best. It will take time, and it can be frustrating, but just as in your garden, once you have the weeds under control, you will reap the fruits of your labor.

Reflection

How can you get more comfortable using your new toolbox to position yourself for opportunities?
How aware are you of your environment and how it can impact your success?
Are you ready to build your Authentic Success Mastermind Group?

Goals

Understand where you are in your journey and understand what you need to do to be positioned for success.

Actions

Develop an action plan to be positioned for success.

CHAPTER 9

Your Authentic Success Roadmap

*"Would you like me to give you a formula for success?
It's quite simple, really: Double your rate of failure.
You are thinking of failure as the enemy of success.
But it isn't at all. You can be discouraged by failure, or
you can learn from it, so go ahead and make mistakes.
Make all you can. Because remember that's where you
will find success."*
–THOMAS J. WATSON

*"What seems to us as bitter trials are often
blessings in disguise."*
–OSCAR WILDE

*"Twenty years from now you will be more disappointed
by the things that you didn't do than by the ones you did
do. So, throw off the bowlines. Sail away from the safe
harbor. Catch the trade winds in your sails.
Explore. Dream. Discover."*
–MARK TWAIN

The world has changed. In the past, people would work hard when
they were young, get into a rhythm as they aged, and then slow down

and slide into retirement. People are living longer, the loyalty level in employer-employee relationships has changed, and there are new opportunities for people to try new things. If you are looking for a traditional career from entry level to retirement, you may have more difficulties than in the past. If you are open to a less traditional career, you may find new opportunities you never thought of.

It is decision time. What do you want to do to become an Authentic Success? If you have been following the recommendations in this book, you have done a lot of work already, and if you are going to become an Authentic Success, you have more work to do. If you are going to stick with the program, you need to uncover what drives you. Think back to a time when you wanted to give up on something. There is a good chance that you did not know or were questioning your purpose. If your purpose is strong enough, you will persevere. If it is not, you will give up.

The process of becoming an Authentic Achiever can be a lot of work. You may be asking if it is worth putting in all of this effort. If you are visualizing the traditional career path, you may be asking, Aren't we closer to the end of our path than the beginning? Life is not necessarily linear. There are stops and starts, U-turns, and bridges to build. If you are thinking you are closer to the end than the beginning, consider that people are living longer, so you may have a lot of time to achieve your goals. With a better understanding of how the body works, better healthcare, and improved sanitation than in the past, people are healthier and can have the opportunity to live longer. There is a good chance you will have access to more opportunities because you may have more time to act on them.

What do you want to do with that time? When Social Security was enacted, people were not living long past 65. They had a couple of years in retirement. Now people are living into their eighties. What would you do with twenty years of retirement? This question is especially relevant if you do not have the money to have a very comfortable lifestyle once you retire.

The earlier you consider this question, the more opportunities you can find, but this question is valid even if you have already retired. What will you be doing when you in five, ten, or even twenty years? If you have the opportunity to do something new, will you be healthy enough to accomplish it? You may be able to function pretty well right now, being very overweight, but do you think the same will be true in twenty years?

Consider what your life will be like when you are older:

§   Will you have the energy to do what you want to do?

§   Will you have the money to do what you want to do?

§   Will you have the support systems?

§   Will you have strong relationships with friends and family?

§   Is your drive strong enough to motivate you through pitfalls?

When you get older, you may want more personal interactions, and they may not be there for you if you don't invest in them now. Harry Chapin's song, "Cats in the Cradle," is about a father who works hard but neglects his family, and when he wants to spend time with his son, his son is too busy. Are you on that path? It would help to do an honest assessment of yourself. Once you have the baseline from the assessment, you can put together a plan to get to where you want to go.

There is no guarantee that we will have a long, healthy life. Any of us can die tomorrow, but it's prudent to plan for the eventuality of living longer. No matter how long we live, we should strive for a fulfilling life. What a fulfilling life means is different for each person, so it is your responsibility to determine what that means to you. Life is challenging, but it can be exciting. It becomes dull and frustrating when you progress without a purpose. You can achieve an Authentic Success when you make a conscious effort to work on your goals and make a regular assessment of your progress.

Even though it is never too late to make a change, the sooner you start, the better. The longer you wait, the more inertia will keep pushing you down the path you are on now. Put a stake in the ground today to strive to make sure you are on the right path. No one wants to sit down at the end of their lives with regrets, saying I could have done this or I should have done that.

Think of your goals as the oxygen mask on an airplane. You need to put on your mask before you help others. Focusing on your goals first is not a selfish act. On the plane, if you pass out from lack of oxygen, you will not be able to help anybody. It is similar to your life in general. If you do not work on your goals first, you will begin to resent the people around you, and you will not be able to help them as effectively because you will be distracted by disappointment, regrets, and dissatisfaction.

I recently saw a reel on social media talking about how soon people forget about us after we die, so we should focus on ourselves. That message did not resonate with me. Hypothetical situations that are outside of our control don't offer a strong enough motivation to achieve big goals. I think about the people who are no longer with us who have had an impact on my life. They have a legacy, so the premise of being forgotten is false in this case.

If you are driven by legacy, then you need to have an impact on people. Preferably, a positive impact. Having an impact takes intentional action. This demonstrated that you can have any purpose and that uncovering what drives you is a personal thing. What other people think of your motivation is not relevant. If you are going to achieve an Authentic Success, you need to determine your motivation.

Without purpose, you can get frustrated, and a sense of dissatisfaction can bleed into your everyday interactions. If that dissatisfaction is noticed by others, you get labeled as the old grumpy person. I know people who are much younger than I who have been labeled as an old, grumpy person. Being grumpy makes you unpleasant to be around and causes opportunities to slip away from you. There is a good chance that if you let it continue, you will find yourself pigeonholed or without a job and having a hard time getting one at the same level. Finding your purpose is essential to maintaining your Performance Image. If you took the time and effort to build your Performance Image, it would be a waste to let bitterness and dissatisfaction bleed through and ruin it.

With all the work you have done thus far, you have a good idea of what it means to be an Authentic Success. It's time to bring it all together and develop your roadmap. You need a roadmap to not only find your destination but to track your progress.

When I was vacationing with my family, we hiked in a national park. We were used to state parks with trails in loops, not long trails that led to other trails. We had gotten lost. We walked outside of the area for which I had maps. We had no idea if we were going in the correct direction. Luckily, we ran into an actual milestone that pointed us in the right direction.

That experience is similar to one many people go through in life. They are plodding along trails and celebrate when they hit milestones, but really have no idea what the milestones mean or even if they are going in the right direction. Those people do not give themselves a map; they just start walking. On the hike mentioned above, we ran low on water, which slowed us down and could have been dangerous. The same can happen in your life journey. Instead of not having water at the right time, you may not have the right skill or enough energy.

You would be well served by a map for the entire journey. It can be destructive to set a goal and then become complacent in mapping your journey. If you do, you can go off track. On the hike, we had a map of the area we wanted to walk in, but we left that area accidentally. Once you reach a goal, you have left the area you mapped out. You are in new territory, and you may need a new map that shows where you want to go next. Even if your goal is to stay where you are, it helps you to understand your position; otherwise, you may start to slip backward and not be as effective. You may start getting frustrated even though you choose to stay where you are. That can result in you losing what you have obtained, and you may experience a setback.

A plan can help to keep you on track. The best goals are written goals. You can refer to your goals and plan if you get lost, just like the map in the woods. You may have a mental image of where you want to go, but if you wander off the path a little bit, having a written map makes it a lot easier to get back on track.

Using your plans effectively can require focus. Focus can ebb and flow, but it does improve with use. Your mind needs as much exercise as your body. We can exercise the mind through activities just like the body. In martial arts, there are sets of movements called kata. These katas are activities that involve the mind and body. To execute them properly, you need to not only memorize the moves and perform them, but you also need to understand them. The moves can be very subtle and confusing. It takes a melding of mind and body to execute them. That is one of the reasons that I love kata. I need to think and move, which helps to keep me sharp.

With these ideas in mind, let's develop a roadmap to your authentic success.

ROADMAP

PART 1: REFLECTION

A common theme in this book is the idea of reflection. As you continue in your journey, you will find that you already have the answers to your questions; you just need to uncover them. You may need a coach, mentor, or trusted advisor to help you uncover your roadmap, but you have the solutions you need already.

Think of your reflection as an interview. You are trying to get someone to reveal the information you need to make your decisions. That person happens to be you. Since this may be a new experience, it helps to start with an organized set of questions. As you get better at it, you can get more conversational. Having a conversation with yourself is much different than negative self-talk. By having an intentional conversation, you can drive the topics and uncover the solutions you need.

"Have you realized that most of your unhappiness in life is due to the fact that you are listening to yourself instead of talking to yourself?"
–Martyn Lloyd-Jones

You may not have the comfort level for a self-conversation. It can help to have an independent third party help guide you. If you can't visualize what that guide would look like, turn to fiction for examples. In many stories, a hero needs to find themselves, and those heroes have guides to help them. Examples include Star Wars–Hero: Luke Skywalker–Guide: Obi-Wan Kenobi; Karate Kid–Hero: Daniel–Guide: Mr. Miyagi; Hunger Games–Hero: Katniss–Guide: Haymitch Abernathy.

Having a guide can provide you a shortcut to an Authentic Success. A coach, mentor, or trusted advisor can guide you as you uncover your solutions. These guidance sessions often start with questions. These questions offer you the opportunity to have a guided reflection. Your guide can help you by asking questions you may not have thought of. This can help you find solutions within yourself that you may never have uncovered on your own.

PART 2: DOCUMENTATION

Have you ever had a great idea while driving, then when you get to your destination, you can't for your life remember what that idea was?

How many great ideas are lost because they are not documented at the time they were thought of? It would be a shame to do all the work of reflection only to have the ideas you generate evaporate into the ether.

As you are reflecting, you will have ideas on how to achieve your goals. It is important to document those ideas for later analysis. There are many ways to document your ideas that you can choose, depending on your comfort level and circumstances. I use a variety of ways to document my ideas, from writing to recording ideas on my phone. I have several apps that I use, and I leave pens and notebooks everywhere.

You should experiment with the different tools out there to determine what works for you. Remember that you will get ideas while driving, while working out, walking your dog, when you are about to fall asleep, when you are talking with other people, and many other scenarios. It can help to have a variety of methods to document your thoughts so you can do it effectively and safely (i.e., while driving).

Documentation is not the time to analyze. It is time to record. Write out your ideas as a stream of consciousness. Just get it recorded. If you start analyzing your idea before you record it, you risk losing details. The analysis is a distraction. Your brain will try to rationalize your idea, especially if you think it is outrageous. It is best to have a complete idea in its raw form rather than a half-forgotten idea that is well organized. The purpose of documentation is to keep you from forgetting your ideas.

When you are intentionally developing ideas, whether it is a brainstorming session or a coaching session, it can be helpful to record the session. There are many tools you can use to record audio or video. There are transcription services and even artificial intelligence tools that can transcribe as you go. This frees you up to think and be creative instead of having to concern yourself with taking notes.

The key to documenting your ideas is catching the nuances. Your best ideas can be buried in the stream of consciousness. If you focus on the loudest voice, you can miss the whispers that contain the treasure. Are all of your ideas going to be good? No! This process is like panning for gold. You gather a big pile that looks like dirt. That is the documentation part. You then wash the dirt in a pan by the river to find and gather the bits of gold. That comes later.

You can't pan for gold without a pile of dirt, and you can't find your next life-changing idea without documenting all your ideas. At first, the process will seem tedious, but once you start getting results and you find the methods that work best for you, it will become a process you integrate into your success plan. No process is perfect, and some ideas will vanish, but your gold is in that pile of ideas you've documented.

PART 3: ORGANIZATION/ANALYSIS

Now you have a big pile of ideas. It is time to organize them and analyze them. There are a few steps you can take to help you organize your ideas and set priorities.

1. When you look through your ideas, you will find that many of the ideas are related to other ideas. As you look through your ideas, gather them by their similarities. I use MS Excel to organize my ideas, but you can organize them however you feel comfortable, even if you write them on separate pieces of paper.

2. Once you have your ideas categorized, write down what they have in common. That common theme is a goal. By organizing your ideas, you have uncovered the goals you want to accomplish.

3. Which of these goals has the most ideas under it? These are the goals you are thinking about most, even if it is in your subconscious. This tells you what is most important to you.

4. Now set your priorities. Just because something is important to you does not make it a priority. There may be things that need to be done first before you can do what is most important to you.

Now that you have organized your ideas, you are ready to develop your plan. However, you will continue to get ideas as you are planning and executing your plan. You need to continue the organizational effort as you get new ideas. I have ideas all the time for actions of varying priorities, and I organize them and add them to my plan based on priority. For example, I had an idea on the structure of this chapter while I was in a meeting. I wrote a note to document the idea, and then I continued the meeting. Once the meeting was over, I reviewed the idea immediately because I thought it was urgent. I determined that it was a good idea, so I added it to my tasking app so I could execute on it when I was writing the following morning. I have other ideas that are residing in notebooks and note-taking apps that will be reviewed later because they are not urgent. We'll get into the apps in the planning section.

Time is like cash flow. You have different amounts at different times. Just as you might wait until you get paid to pay your bills, you may need to wait to review your ideas until a later time. If you get a collection notice from a bill you forgot to pay, you may not wait until payday, pay the bill, and skip eating out that week. The same works for your ideas. I thought my book idea was important enough to postpone other tasks to analyze, but I am scheduling them for a future date.

It is prudent to schedule times to review your ideas. If you wait too long, you may not recognize what you wrote. There have been times when I wrote down ideas to look at them later, and when I reviewed them, I had no idea what I meant. There have been other times when I've looked at an idea and been inspired to document even more ideas. Having regular review times can help you minimize idea loss while allowing you to enhance other ideas.

You will find some great ideas, some bad ideas, and some ideas that need additional research. As you analyze, you can organize the ideas. I use the FAT organization system.

F–File away low-priority ideas and ideas that need more research

A–Act on the high-priority, good ideas

T–Trash the bad ideas

This is a simple system that is easy to use and remember. I also use it for email management.

How you prioritize your ideas depends on your goals and your work style. You will need to develop a prioritization regime that works for you. You can work with your coach to help you design a personalized plan. There are many tools you can use to help you organize and analyze. I use a variety of things from pen and paper to organization apps. Try not to get seduced by the technology. Use what you are comfortable with, and that makes you efficient. The process is more important than the tools.

PROCESS

- § Gathering your ideas
- § Organizing those ideas
- § Analyzing the ideas
- § Determining which ideas are worth pursuing
- § Trashing the bad ideas
- § Prioritizing your good ideas

This process can be done with a pen and paper. Once you have the process down, you might find that the introduction of technology will make you more effective, but tech does not replace the process.

Once you get to the point that you trust the process, it can become a habit where you regularly review and prioritize your ideas. There will be times when other priorities will get in the way of organizing and analyzing your ideas. Don't stress over it. You documented your ideas, and they will wait for you. There are times when I've forgotten about notebooks and come back to them months or even years later, only to find great ideas and act on them. The analysis took more time because I had to remember what I meant when I originally documented my ideas, but I still found valuable ideas that I was able to put into action.

PART 4: PLANNING

This process will generate a lot of ideas. You will find the process inspiring but also overwhelming. When you see a giant pile of ideas, no matter how well they are prioritized, it is hard to know where to start, and you may doubt whether you can accomplish them. The key to bringing your ideas to fruition is an effective plan.

I have found a way to integrate a plan into your everyday life. In the past, I had complex written plans, like the ones I created for work, but I never followed them in the long term. I would proceed in fits and starts, developing the plan, sort of following it, revising the plan, and repeating the process. That path was frustrating and ineffective. Through experimentation, I found that the combination of calendaring, task management, and note-taking, combined with a simple overall plan, works best.

Simple Overall Plan

When you were organizing your ideas, you did most of the work for the plan. You have converted your ideas into goals, and you have set priorities. You now know what you want to do and what is most important to you. This is the foundation of your plan. Now look at your goals and priorities and find patterns. What do your groups of goals and priorities have in common? You may find several patterns. When I performed this exercise, I saw goals like writing books, coaching people, and teaching workshops, which showed the pattern of educating people. That was my first and highest priority pattern. Other goals showed me that I wanted to help people build companies and some other patterns.

The patterns uncovered my overall objectives, the ideas are the goals I want to accomplish, and how they should be prioritized. Now, we need to schedule actions. I attended a time management seminar twenty years ago that significantly impacted how I approach achieving my goals. The number one lesson I learned was to keep all scheduling in one place. If you use Outlook at work for your work scheduling, a calendar on your refrigerator at home for your family activities, and a plan on your desk in your home office for your plan, you will find yourself missing things and falling behind.

There are many ways to centralize your scheduling, but I find my phone to be the best place to do it. The cell phone has become a central part of our lives, which is why I use it as my central repository. Many apps can be used across platforms, so you can access them from your computers, tablets, and phones. Many companies restrict the addition of apps on their equipment, and you may not want your employer to know what you are doing outside of work, so it may be prudent to leave it off your employer's equipment. They do have the right to see the information on the machine, even if it is private to you.

This is another time to avoid getting seduced by technology. I know people who use paper planning solutions who successfully manage their plans and priorities. Whether high or low tech, there are a few tools I find essential to building your Authentic Success Plan. The Authentic Success Plan template is broken into three parts: calendaring, task management, and note-taking. I have found apps that work for me, and I recommend that you research the apps available for your phone and determine what works best for you.

When calendaring, include all your activities, even if they are recorded elsewhere. Your life is multifaceted, so you have multiple sources of time requirements. Having them all in one place lets you see the whole picture of your schedule, so you always know what you need to do. Some apps allow you to connect to other calendars, so they are automatically updated from all your sources.

Task management is the second part of planning. You might be wondering why you don't just use your calendar to monitor your tasks. If you do, it can make you appear to have no time during the day. I recommend using your calendar only for things that need to be completed at specific times. If you want to complete a task but can do so at any time during the day, the task management system is a better resource.

Task Management apps can help you prioritize your tasks, monitor your progress, allow you to re-prioritize as things change, and let you see what you have in store in the future.

Remember, just because you aren't in the reflection stage doesn't mean you won't get new ideas. As you are planning, you will get new ideas. Having a notetaking system near you at all times will help you capture the ideas for later review. I have a note-taking app that allows me to type or dictate notes to my phone and computer. I also rely on paper notes.

You have chosen your tools; it is time to use them. You have an organized, prioritized set of ideas, tasks, and goals. Your list will probably exceed the amount of time you have right now to work on it all. It is time to lay out your execution plan. Enter your tasks into your task management system. You may have tasks that you won't look at for months. That's okay. You are working on your priorities first. I have tasks that are scheduled for next year. If you have appointments associated with your tasks, add them to your calendar. Once you have your tasks scheduled, you are ready to act.

PART 6: EXECUTION

You have done a lot of preparation. You have a plan. Now it is time to act. You may find yourself feeling anxious or doubting your plan; that's natural.

If you have done a thorough job in developing your Authentic Success Plan, you will be able to see your work, personal, and primary tasks and calendar items together. The tasks are achievable, but probably a challenge. Until you build the habits around the additional work you will be doing, you will feel extra busy. As you get used to it, the tasks will feel normal, and you will get more efficient. You will get more done in less time.

The key is to act. It can be difficult, but to reach an Authentic Success, you need to break through the I can't barrier. Your brain will tell you that you have reached your limits before you reach your limits. Like lifting weights, your task management will get stronger the harder tasks you accomplish. Each task will teach you something about execution, and you will get better at it over time.

PART 7: EVALUATION

At work, your boss probably gives you an evaluation at least once a year. If it's only once a year, it's likely just to provide reasons for or against a pay increase. However, there are times when you will learn something about your performance in the evaluation. When there is an effective evaluation process, the employee learns how to improve and gets guidance as they improve.

With this process, you are playing both sides of the evaluation. You are evaluating and being evaluated. Since you aren't an independent evaluator, you may be too hard or easy on yourself when evaluating your performance. If you start feeling bad about yourself, you are being too hard on yourself, and if you aren't finding any lessons, you are probably being too easy.

If you are uncomfortable with the evaluation process, a coach can help you. As an independent observer, they can help you perform a self-evaluation and set limits so you aren't too hard or soft on yourself. Many coaches have tools that can help you through the process and give you insights that could take you years to learn on your own.

In the end, this is your plan. You decide how to execute it. If you find yourself overwhelmed, you may have added too many tasks up front. You can reschedule some to later times. If you feel you can do more, you can reschedule to a more aggressive pace.

Another factor to consider when evaluating your progress is a life change. Things happen that are out of your control, and these can impact your task management and change your priorities. It's ok to postpone tasks as priorities change. After the pandemic, I had a period of inconsistent employment. I lost my full-time job, and I needed to take a series of contract positions and consulting assignments just to stay afloat. I needed to postpone everything but job search so I could get a stable income. Once that was accomplished, I reevaluated my tasks and started the process again.

PART 8: REFRAMING

Plans are written on paper, not carved in stone. Situations change. Priorities change. A static plan is not an effective plan. That does not mean you should change on a whim. Thoughtful, intentional changes to your plan will help you succeed faster. The question is, how do you know when to change?

I like to use the OODA Loop to determine when to make changes. United States Air Force fighter pilot and military strategist Colonel John Boyd developed a decision-making tool called the OODA Loop. The OODA Loop has four steps:

1. Observe

2. Orient

3. Decide

4. Act.

It's great for quick decisions:

1. What's happening?

2. How does it impact your goals and strategy?

3. What do you need to do to achieve your goals?

4. Do it!

I use the OODA Loop so often that I don't even realize it. I recommend this tool because it is straightforward and effective. It works on everything from avoiding traffic to achieving your biggest goals.

An example of my use of the OODA Loop was my analysis of my unemployment:

Observe: I had a number of goals that would help me in my career and life in general, but my income was curtailed by unemployment, and I had expenses and responsibilities that I needed to address.

Orient: If I wanted to address my expenses and responsibilities, I needed to address my unemployment. The best way to do that was to put everything aside except looking for a job.

Decide: I put aside everything other than finding income-producing employment.

Act: I put 100 percent effort into getting a job until I found stable employment.

Once I found employment, I reframed again and slowly got back on track with my other goals.

You may find yourself being influenced by sunk costs and inertia, making you resistant to change. A coach can help you work through what your next steps should be.

PART 9: OVERCOME THE EGO OBSTACLE

When sunk costs and inertia influence you, you can become an obstacle to your own success. You can be your own worst enemy. I read a book a while ago that talked about ego. It compared the ego to the airbag in a car. The ego is there to protect your self-esteem. Like an airbag, it helps you when you crash, keeping the "life crash" from destroying your confidence. However, if our egos are out of control, they become obstacles to our success. Think about trying to drive with your airbag always deployed. You are protected from a crash, but you cannot see the road. You just see the airbag (your ego). You have created a self-imposed obstacle by relying on your ego to protect you.

How will an out-of-control ego affect you?

§ Ego can keep you from learning from younger people or people that you don't particularly like.

§ Ego pushes you to go it alone.

§ Ego can keep you from writing plans.

§ Ego can keep you from taking classes.

§ Ego can make you feel like you don't need to put in the extra effort.

§ Ego can also keep you from taking risks.

§ Ego is afraid of failure.

If there is a risky plan that has a reasonable chance of success, you (your ego) may talk yourself out of it for fear of failure. An established path is comfortable. You know it and have a good idea of what will happen when you follow it. Trying something new does not give you that sense of security. You won't know your way around this new path as well as the old. There is a good chance you will make mistakes, and you may fail.

It helps to reflect honestly on where you are, where you want to go, and what you are willing to give up to get there.

§ Are you willing to give up two hours of sleep every night to wake up early and read, exercise, or write a book?

§ Are you willing to forgo a steady income to try starting a business?

§ Are you willing to miss some of your family events to get more production, or are you willing to give up some production to make it to your family event?

§   Are you willing to give up watching your favorite TV show to take a class and do homework?

§   Are you willing to do what it takes to get ahead, make sacrifices?

§   **Do you want to be an Authentic Achiever?**

PART 10: COMMIT TO AN AUTHENTIC SUCCESS

Suppose you are willing to commit to becoming an Authentic Achiever. In that case, it helps to imagine a clear picture of why you are doing it and understand the benefits, because you need to commit to the future self at the cost of the present self. The perceived benefit of immediate satisfaction from eating a cookie can be more powerful than the perceived benefit of being fit and healthy later. Being able to see the benefits of being fit and healthy and having the discipline to put the cookie down is essential to success. The one flaw to this analogy is that it gives the impression of suffering now for benefits later. A disciplined approach does not have to be unpleasant. Your path to becoming an Authentic Achiever can and really should be a satisfying journey. Life is too short for anything else.

You have probably heard that money cannot buy happiness. It can, however, buy peace of mind. The key to success, however, is not money. It is happiness. If you can bring happiness to yourself and those around you, you are an Authentic Success. How you accomplish that success is a very personal thing, and even the definition of happiness is yours alone. In our society, money plays a significant role in determining success. It helps to be able to pay your bills. Even if your goal is to help the community and you have taken a vow of poverty, money is integral to helping you serve the community.

If you are going to achieve an Authentic Success, you need some foundational resources: shelter, food, water, etc. All those things take money. Living off the grid, building your own house, getting your own water, and hunting or growing your own food is very challenging. Because of our population and the laws around the use of open space, the opportunity to live off the grid is rare. Plus, we don't necessarily have the required skills to do it, and you would be giving up many of the things that keep us healthy longer. Food preservation, refrigeration, healthcare, and medicine all cost money. Then, if we want to live beyond the basics of adding in education, leisure time, and luxuries, we need more money.

Not to belabor the point, but we need money in our society if we are going to achieve our goals. Whether we use it for ourselves or others, we need it. The key is not to get obsessed with money. Money is like air in our society. If we don't have it and we need it, we panic. If you have ever been underwater too long, you start to get the burning feeling in your lungs, and you panic. The same can happen when your bills come in, and you don't have enough to cover them. You can panic.

It's best to control your money. That means knowing exactly how much you make and exactly how much you spend. With direct deposit, it can be easy to miss key transactions. You may not even check to make sure you are being paid what you are owed. When was the last time you confirmed your paycheck was accurate? Do you just assume that the check is correct? Mistakes happen. I know someone who had a mistake made on their bonus. He was owed thousands of dollars more than he received. He caught the mistake, and it was corrected. If it is a smaller amount, we might not catch it so easily, and that can accumulate over time.

It also helps to check your expenses. Your credit card statements are the first place to check. You may have memberships or subscriptions that you don't use. Unused services are just throwing away money. That is money that can go to paying other bills or savings. There may be ways to cut costs without having a big impact on your lifestyle.

Throughout the book, I recommend a holistic approach to success. A singular path to success can leave you feeling empty because you are not addressing all of your needs. Life balance is important. A friend of mine teaches a time management course, and he has some great tips on time management. Basic things like saving your work on your computer. If you work for two hours on your computer and you lose the work because you didn't save it, you've lost two hours of your life that you can't get back. The same goes for other parts of your life. If you only focus on work and neglect your personal life, you can lose a source of happiness and peace. A balanced life can help you achieve Authentic Success. It also helps to have something you do outside of work. I enjoy martial arts, and I am starting to hike. Part of my Authentic Success is leisure and family activities. I always tried to be there for my family, but I had to provide for them. I had very time-consuming jobs, and I missed a lot of personal milestones. I was there for my family, but not as much as I could have been. I ran myself ragged and was often tired. As in my career, I made mistakes outside of work. I did not spend enough time on non-work items. I was not living a balanced life.

Balanced does not mean fifty-fifty, and it is not a constant. There will be times when work needs to come first so that you can pay your bills. There is also a time when your personal time comes first, when there's a crisis or something really special happening. There may also be a time when you need time for yourself. You need to consider all these things when planning your path to an Authentic Success. Success is not just the destination; it is the path. You need to be satisfied along the way. If you are miserable on your path to success, you probably won't feel too successful. Not every day is going to be great, but you should have a sense of hope and excitement when you're pursuing your Authentic Success.

My wife and I had a definition of success that was different from many of our peers. We decided that she would stay home as the kids were growing up. If I do the math, that decision cost us well over a million dollars. That is a lot of money. Not having that money does not make us less successful. We had the opportunity to raise our kids the way we wanted to, and that was an Authentic Success to us. Now that my children are grown up, our situation has changed, and I have some goals I postponed that I am now working to achieve. I look back at the successes and failures and am satisfied. I continue to strive to be an Authentic Success so I can look back twenty years from now and have the same reaction.

Reflection

Where are you in your journey?
How do you define success?
What is holding you back?

Goals

Document what you need to accomplish to achieve the success you defined.

Actions

Take your reflections, find the tools you are comfortable with, and develop your plan.

CHAPTER 10

Living the Life You Deserve

"Don't be afraid to give up the good to go for the great."
–John D. Rockefeller

"Keep on going, and the chances are that you will stumble on something, perhaps when you are least expecting it. I never heard of anyone ever stumbling on something sitting down."
–Charles F. Kettering

"Success is just a war of attrition. Sure, there's an element of talent you should probably possess. But if you just stick around long enough, eventually something is going to happen."
–Dax Shepard

As your life progresses and you evolve, your priorities are going to evolve too. These changes will change your goals and what you are willing to do to achieve them. You might find yourself with new responsibilities or health challenges. All these things can change your definition of an Authentic Success, and those changes require changes to your plan. The question is, when is it appropriate to make those changes? If you make frequent changes, you won't be able to build momentum or achieve efficiencies. You can use the OODA loop as discussed in the last chapter to help you with this decision-making.

Examples of when changes can be made are:

§   Your Annual Review

§   A material life setback: The loss of a job, a health challenge, a significant financial setback

§   A material life breakthrough: A promotion, a new opportunity, a financial boon

The point is to only make changes with intention. Your life changes, so you need to keep up while balancing consistency with adaptation.

Fast forward, ten, twenty, thirty years. Where will you be? The concept of retirement has evolved as people are living longer. You may be working past the traditional retirement age. It may be by choice or necessity. You may need to work. You probably don't have millions in the bank waiting for you to finally end your career and live comfortably. You need to consider the possibility that you may outlive your money if you don't have a plan. Many people don't plan adequately for their retirement. I have been guilty of that. There are just so many other obligations and expenses that it can be hard to start saving early enough, so that by the time you reach your fifties, you have confidence that you will be able to retire within the next ten-plus years.

There are fewer organizations that offer pensions, and even fewer opportunities to stay at one company long enough to get vested in that pension. You are on your own when it comes to your retirement. We pay into Social Security, but most likely, if you rely on Social Security, your quality of life will decrease dramatically. You need to be able to provide for yourself and your family, even after reaching retirement age.

This future need is a good reason to invest in your present health and energy. Even if you have a perfect pension or savings, life happens. Pension funds go bankrupt; savings are lost. You need to be healthy to retain the ability to work if needed. There is no downside to this plan. If your retirement goes well, you will have more energy to do what you want to do comfortably. Travelling takes energy. Hobbies take energy. Watching grandkids takes energy. If you plan for the eventuality that you will need to work, even if you don't need to work, you will be better off.

If you have a solid retirement plan, you may need to work just for your peace of mind. People dream of retirement, doing nothing, and relaxing. Unfortunately, that can be more pleasant in dreams than in reality. Doing nothing can be boring. Just doing hobbies and busy work can be unsatisfying. People like to be productive. They enjoy doing things that hold meaning. People actually like to work. Bringing home a paycheck is satisfying. When that opportunity is no longer available, it can have a negative impact on self-esteem.

I am at a stage of life where I have been able to witness the impact of a loss of purpose after retirement. I knew an older couple who had retired and had a pension. The husband was under the impression that if he did any more work and paid more into Social Security, he risked losing his health insurance, being forced onto Medicare, and somehow nullifying parts of his retirement plan. It may have been true, but he never talked to an expert to see if there were ways to get around it.

Over time, they got bored, and hobbies became more frustrating than pleasurable. Then, the grandchildren came, and they had a new purpose. They concentrated their life on supporting the grandchildren. As the grandchildren got older and had other activities that kept them from the grandparents, the purpose started to fade again, and boredom and frustration returned.

Purpose can give you the direction and motivation to continue working toward your goals at any age.

The mind can get just as flabby as the body. To maintain mental fitness, it helps to engage in both intellectual and physical activities.

Many of our capacities decline with age. They decline faster when we don't use them. Our minds and bodies atrophy when we are not active. To continue the canoeing-upriver analogy, as we age, we get closer to the rapids. It takes more effort to fight the current, and we get pushed back faster than we did before. We need to fight hard to stay in shape. We need to fight hard to keep our minds sharp. There will come a time when the rapids are stronger than our paddling, so that we will get pushed backward. Our job is to delay that if possible. Our job is to stay in condition to keep paddling.

Having the ability to continue reaching our goals is a good reason to do all the things we talk about in this book. You will be able to persevere longer and take advantage of opportunities that your peers are too tired or afraid to take on.

The whole premise of being an Authentic Success is taking advantage of opportunities even if they come later than you may have expected; to be successful when your peers have given up, to work harder when others are slowing down, and to overcome past mistakes and challenges.

The path to an Authentic Success is rarely a straight line. There are twists and turns, ups and downs. You will still face challenges, but you will just be more prepared to address them successfully. A challenge many people face in their careers is being passed over for promotion. You have probably been in a company where a younger person is promoted instead of an older person who has "paid their dues". It may have been you. Being passed over can appear to be a signal to most people that they have missed the boat. They see the missed opportunity as the end of their growth potential, which can lead to a negative shift in their self-worth. They may believe that they have given it their all and that they did not make the cut.

This belief can be explained with a sports analogy. If you were involved in a childhood sport like Little League Baseball and you experienced success, then you played in high school, and you may have found out that there are a lot of better players. If you then went to college and did not make the sports team, your competitive sports career may have been over. If you use that sports path as a model for your career, you can miss opportunities because that is not how your career works. You are able to make changes and take advantage of new opportunities.

You do not need the specific talents that a sport requires to be successful in a career. All career paths are much more diverse than a sports path. You are not limited as you are in sports. You can go off in many different directions, and the definition of success is also different. Success is not always about hitting the most balls or getting the most strikeouts. Your career might be to get the other team to hit more balls. Careers offer more opportunities than school and professional sports. There will be times that you don't make the cut in the short term, but there are plenty of ways to get beyond that. Think of my sick day story. If I let the sick day situation stall my career, you would not be reading this book now. You have the same opportunity to reach your career goals.

Your journey to success never needs to end. Your priorities will change over time, and you may have different goals, but there is no reason for you to stop striving to get where you want to go.

§   People run marathons when they are seventy

§   Some people work in their eighties and like it

§   People enjoy time with their grandkids and their great grandkids

§   People recover from illness

§   People enjoy life

If they can do it, you can do it!

If you have committed to being an Authentic Achiever, it's decision time.

§   Who do you want to be?

§   How do you want to live?

§   Are you willing to commit to the process?

If you're ready, it's time to create a plan to achieve your goals.

§   Observe—where are you in terms of achieving your goals

§   Orient—How can you get from where you are now to you goal

§   Decide—What are you willing to do to achieve your goals

§   Act—Go out and do it!

Remember the river analogy. Life is always pushing us back down the river. It may seem at times that you are riding a wave, but that ride is a result of your effort. Success does not just happen. You accomplish it. **You do it**. Some people ride on the coattails of others. Some of those people may even be dragged to success. If you find a trailblazer (a person who drives toward their goals) who shares similar goals as you, that can be your easiest path, and you may want to grab on to their coattails and hang on for dear life.

An example of grabbing the coattails is working for an energetic entrepreneur. This is a situation where you may need to let go of your ego. If a younger entrepreneur has a fast-growing company, they may need an experienced person to assist them. You, as an Authentic Achiever, can be a perfect match. You have the experience and can fill the gaps in experience for the company. You can grow with the company as the entrepreneur advances. This type of opportunity can be very exciting and profitable.

As we've discussed, your ego, although useful, needs to be controlled. It helps to let your ego accept the possibility of failure or the idea of working for someone who may be significantly younger than you. You can have fun, be the oldest person in the company, and be successful. Sometimes you need to make the leap. It can be scary, but if you continue doing what you're doing, you'll continue to get what you're getting. Remember that you may not need to jump in with both feet. You may be able to start off as a consultant and work part-time while keeping your day job until you are sure the opportunity is right for you.

No matter how old you get or what condition your life is in, always set goals and have a plan. If you successfully sail around the world, you don't want to crash into the rocks at the last port because you threw away your map. On the other hand, if you have been stuck in the harbor for years, you may find that looking at your map will allow you to get out and sail the ocean.

Goals and plans provide purpose. A purpose can motivate you to complete tasks you don't necessarily want to do. If you work in an environment with forced overtime or very time-sensitive deliverables, you have probably given up some of your goals for someone else's. You worked longer instead of having dinner with your family or playing softball or whatever you want to do. Giving time that can be used to build your own Authentic Success, instead of building someone else's, can be very discouraging. Since people tend to be result-focused, when you don't have an intentional plan to achieve your goals, you may end up focusing on other people's goals when they have a plan you can follow.

Your perspective on what you are working on is also important. When I was younger, I would take holiday work hours whenever I could. Why? I got paid more on those days. Other people would complain about having to work, and I would offer to cover for them. At the time, I was looking for more cash, and I could spend time with my family after work. I was achieving my goal through my working holidays. When I got older, my goals changed, and I no longer wanted to work holidays, so I made a conscious decision to get a job with holidays off.

Since your priorities change as you evolve, and you live in an ever-changing, dynamic environment, you need to think strategically to remain sharp. Your mind needs to be able to work through problems quickly and efficiently. Thinking quickly does not mean acting impulsively. Sometimes you may need a few days to think about something. That does not mean waiting two days and making a poorly thought-out, rushed decision. All the efforts you have made to become an Authentic Achiever is helpful only if you take action based on them. If you read hundreds of books but cannot use the knowledge gained, you only read them for recreation. You need to be able to use the information.

There is no endpoint in your journey to an Authentic Success. The success lies in the journey, not at the end. If you want to live the Authentic Success lifestyle and keep reaching new levels of success, you must keep taking action. Execution is the key. Going beyond what is expected, getting things done, and getting them done well. You need to keep going. Continuing with our canoeing upriver theme, if you read books on how to row efficiently but continue to slap the water with your oar, you will not get anywhere, or worse, you will slide backward. Considering your goals and learning new skills is the first step. You need to put those skills into practice. As you gain new skills and experiences, integrating them into your action plan will make you a more effective achiever.

When we think about executing plans and needing energy, we may think of physical activities, but mental activities can be as demanding as physical ones. You cannot go from playing checkers to becoming a chess master. You need to learn new skills and then apply them. Changing from a game with one type of piece with a set way, like checkers, to chess that has you using multiple piece types, all of which move differently, adds a layer of complexity that takes practice to accomplish. As you progress on your path to Authentic Success, you will find that your life path and goals will become more complex than before. In chess, you can practice outside of competition. You can play against a computer or training partners before you go out and play for real. It is more challenging to apply in real life. You can't practice a sales campaign before you execute it. There are no do-overs when you are performing surgery.

You need to be ready to play every day. This state of readiness is where your experience comes in. Think of your past as practice for today. You acted or didn't in the past, and that is behind you. It is like a practice session for today. That is not to say there are no consequences from your past. If you make big enough mistakes, you will need to correct or atone for them. That is like practice, too. Let's use physical practice for this example. If you are a star athlete and are about to compete in the Olympics, you need to be at the top of your game. You practice constantly and push yourself. In a practice session a couple of weeks before your competition, you tear a cartilage in your knee. What happens? It was just practice, not competition, does it count? Of course, it does. You can be out of the competition or, at best, have limited ability when you compete.

Think of your life that way. Every day is practice for the next, but those practices have consequences. A mistake in practice can hinder you or put you out of the game entirely. If you convert the Authentic Success process into a lifestyle, you will be able to have continued success throughout your life. A great example is education.

Education does not stop when you get a degree. I hear a lot of people disparage education because they didn't apply what they learned as they progressed through their careers. The thing is, they learned how to do their job somewhere. If they know how to do their job and realize they didn't learn it in school, they must have learned it somewhere else. They probably learned it by accident, meaning they did not intentionally seek out the information; they just learned it as they went along.

People can progress by learning without a plan, but they have a lower chance of reaching their full potential. To explain the concept, we used an example of a gold mine. The gold vein was three feet away when the miner quit, and another used an expert to find it. Your education is the same. A better approach to your current method may be just one magazine article or one book away.

§   It may be something that makes you more efficient at work, so you can come home an hour earlier to spend time with your family.

§   It may be something that introduces you to an activity that changes your life. You may find that one paragraph that inspires you to carry on those last hundred steps to the peak of the mountain.

There will be a time when our minds will start to fail us, just as our bodies will. As Authentic Achievers, we should try to delay that as long as possible. If you think back to our discussion on looking back twenty years from now, think about how you would feel about not achieving goals. You should try to get as many of our goals accomplished as possible while enjoying the journey. I mentioned earlier that we should look at the past as practice. I did not say we should look at today as practice. Today is the big game. Today counts. We may have an injury from yesterday's practice, literal or metaphorical, so we will need to adapt to those difficulties to move forward. Practice is over, and we need to play today.

As an Authentic Achiever, think of yourself as an Olympic athlete. You see those athletes compete with injuries all the time. There was an Olympic gymnast who got a gold medal even though she was competing with a broken ankle. Did her competitors give her a break, or did the judges feel bad for her and go easy on her? No, she gritted through the pain and used all her experience and guts to push through and get the job done.

That gymnast was young, but your level of experience is greater, which gives you an advantage. You have more experiences to pull from in your journey. Many of us have the equivalent of a hangnail, and we are bowing out when people with metaphorical broken bones are moving forward. If you continue to learn and put into practice what you learned, you have the opportunity for greatness.

Let's reflect:

What is the status of your Performance Image now?

1. If you have no mistakes that have long-lasting consequences, congratulations, you are ready to move forward with fewer obstacles.

2. If you have the equivalent of being fired from your job, take the time to acknowledge the failure and enhance the area of weakness that got you fired, then get back in the game.

3. If you severely damaged your reputation or had to spend time in jail, you will have the toughest time, but you can still get the gold medal.

The great thing about life is that it is not a single competition like the Olympics. You don't need to wait four years to compete again. You get to play again the next day, and you get to improve. If you have had serious setbacks, you can still succeed by refocusing and committing yourself to your own success. I watched as some of my peers seemed to effortlessly advance to higher levels of management, while I was stuck in the middle. It wasn't until I looked closer and saw the full picture that I understood. I was trying to apply my experiences to understand their successes. I was projecting my accomplishments onto them, and it was skewing my perception of why they were succeeding in places where I was not. It turned out that many of the people whom I thought were successes were not Authentic Achievers when measured against my personal definition of success. Each of those people had a different idea of success, which did not necessarily align with my definition.

"Success is not a destination, it's a journey."
—Zig Ziglar

§   Are you ready to achieve an Authentic Success?

§   Do you understand what you want from life?

§   Are you willing to strive to achieve the life you want?

If so, you are ready to achieve an Authentic Success. It's a good idea to spend the time you need to determine what you want and put together a plan of how to get it. Even if it's just to go fishing on Saturday.

I had a job that was very challenging and had such a long commute that every weekday was 100 percent dedicated to my job at the expense of social and recreational activities, and in getting personal business done. I had so much personal business to get done on Saturday that I would never have time for other activities. I've discussed it with friends and family. We always said we should make plans to get together, but it didn't happen until I made the changes. I needed to make time to do the things that would help me achieve my Authentic Success. We weren't put on this planet to make a living; we need to make a life. That is an authentic success. Success is that journey.

I know this seems hard, and you may be asking yourself: Why should you do it? If you don't do it, you may always be a victim of your own inertia, with a focus on other people's goals rather than your own. People tend to follow the path of least resistance and following that path builds inertia. That is the path to disappointment and bitterness.

People tend to regret the things they didn't do rather than the things they did. Don't get me wrong, everyone has done things they regret, but it will probably be the things that you did not do that will haunt you. You have probably heard of a bucket list, a list of the things we want to do before we "kick the bucket." That list will become one of two things. It can be a wish list that turns into regret, or it can become a plan that turns into a satisfying life.

We have covered a lot of material. Let's connect the dots. How can you position yourself for an Authentic Success Lifestyle?

§　**The Turbocharged Mindset:** Develop a resilient goal achievement mindset that gives you the foundation you need to achieve an Authentic Success.

§　**Performance Image:** Be conscious of how people (including yourself) see you and make an effort to develop an image that maximizes your ability to succeed.

§　**The Intentionally Sharpened Mind:** Develop a purposeful learning plan and become a lifelong learner, equipping yourself with the skills necessary to achieve your goals.

§　**The Technology Advantage:** Stay on top of technological advances and add appropriate tools to your toolbox to keep you efficient and relevant.

§　**Using Your Success Toolbox:** Progress takes action. The tools you have developed while reading this book will help you take action more effectively and with more confidence.

Our lifestyle choices go beyond achieving goals. We need to feel good about ourselves to be happy. It is hard to feel good about ourselves when we are tired all the time, feel out of shape, and maybe yearn for the times when we were younger and more active. It is not empowering to have to unbutton your pants to tie your shoes. It is certainly not empowering to suffer from heart disease or diabetes or any of the other health issues that can be caused by being overweight.

We invest money for our retirement. Shouldn't we invest in our health? What is the point of saving money to travel after you retire if you are too sick and tired to travel? You need well-rounded thoughts about success. If you work like crazy to achieve a good retirement but neglect your health, what do you have? You may have a lot you want to accomplish, and you need time to do it. To have that time, you need to invest in yourself. It helps to intentionally invest in your body the same way you invest in your 401K. You need your body to carry you through your life.

The whole point of this book is that you are never too old to achieve your goals. You may not be a professional baseball player when you are fifty, but there are opportunities to play baseball. You may not be a professional fighter at sixty, but you can get a black belt in martial arts. You may not be the president of a major corporation, but you can run your own business.

It is really important to understand the "why" behind a destination. I say 'destination, not goal,' because the true goal is often hidden behind the destination. When we understand what we want, we stop being blinded by the destination and focus on the goal. The destination can be a distraction. It is the thing excuses are made of. I could have gone to Harvard, but I couldn't afford it. I could have been a star pitcher, but I hurt my shoulder. I could have done this or that. Life throws you curveballs. You did not get to the destination. What goal were you trying to accomplish?

We have to accept that life puts us all in different places:

§   You may not have all the same advantages as others.

§   You may need to work harder than others to get to a certain level.

§   You may not have many paths available to others.

§   You may have made a mistake so egregious that your reputation is damaged.

When it comes to achieving goals, we are not on a level playing field, and we must simply accept this reality.

The key to success is actually knowing your goal and not being distracted by destinations. When I was in college, I started networking to get a job. I did all the "right things". I met people, learned what I needed to do, and I went to my interviews. Everything was going well until all the banks I met with started going out of business. It was the S&L Crisis, and all my work opportunities went out the window. I was stuck scrambling for another job.

That economic situation caused me to have a lot of bumps in my road to success. The key was that I kept focused on my goal of being successful in my own way. At times, my path was very nebulous. Even just dreaming about being a millionaire while driving in my car, I always knew I could be successful. My path was a wandering one, and over time, I learned what success meant to me. I learned that it was not always about money, but that money was an important factor. I never stopped learning. I am a voracious reader. I take classes. I have coaches. I have had mentors, too.

By reading this book, you have shown a desire and a commitment to finding your success. You have probably hit a bunch of bumps in the road and may even be a bit discouraged. Commit to exercising your body and brain. Really understand what you want your goals to be. Learn the skills you need to learn and go out and reach your goals.

You have such great potential. I hope you give yourself permission to reach your full potential.

Thank you for reading. If you enjoyed this book, please rate it on Amazon.com.

Good Luck on your journey!
You're not too old, and it's not too late!

If you have questions when reading the book, go to **www. AnAuthenticSuccess.com** and submit them.

About the Author

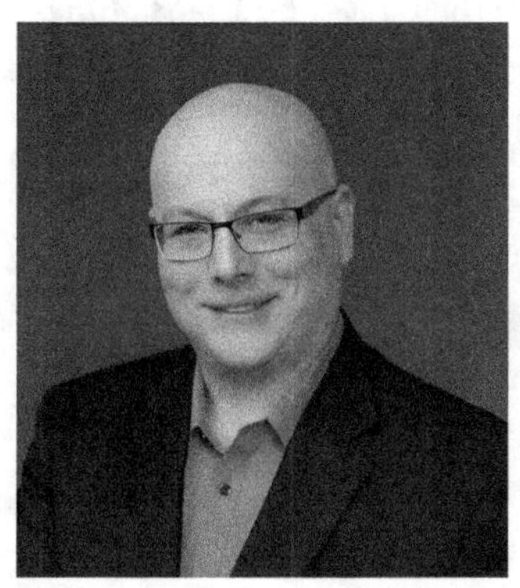 **Chad C. Betz** is a respected financial services executive, professional development speaker, and executive coach. Chad is recognized by C-suite executives, peers, and teams for his confident leadership, analytical skill, and ability to solve complex problems under pressure. His approach blends technical expertise with a deep understanding of human motivation and organizational behavior.

Throughout his career, Chad has led high-performing teams. His core strengths include strategic planning and performance optimization, and his professional philosophy centers on disciplined leadership and continuous improvement. He has developed frameworks and performance measures that enhance organizational effectiveness while fostering human potential. As a seasoned communicator and trusted advisor, Chad has designed and given presentations for domestic and international audiences.

In addition to his corporate work, Chad volunteers his time to help professional job seekers revitalize their job searches using the concepts and strategies outlined in his books. Through workshops, presentations, and mentoring, he equips individuals, particularly those facing mid-career transitions, with the tools to rebuild confidence, realign goals, and reignite purpose.

Chad holds a Master of Arts in economics from Trinity College and a Bachelor of Science in economics and business administration from Sacred Heart University. A husband, father, and martial artist currently studying Goju Ryu, he believes success is achieved through continuous learning, discipline, and purpose.

He is the author of *The Second Mouse Gets the Cheese!*, *Late Bloomer: It's Not Too Late to Succeed!*, and *Expertise Expedition: Excursions into New Careers*. His works inspire readers to redefine success, embrace resilience, and pursue meaningful growth at every stage of life.